A HISTORY LOVER'S GUIDE TO
BERGEN COUNTY

A HISTORY LOVER'S GUIDE TO

BERGEN COUNTY

BOB NESOFF AND HOWARD JOSEPH COHN

Published by The History Press
Charleston, SC
www.historypress.com

All images are from the authors' collections except those as otherwise noted.

First published 2022

Manufactured in the United States

ISBN 9781467147811

Library of Congress Control Number: 2022937938

Notice: The information in this book is true and complete to the best of our knowledge. It is offered without guarantee on the part of the authors or The History Press. The authors and The History Press disclaim all liability in connection with the use of this book.

CONTENTS

FOREWORD

New Jersey is known as the "Gateway to the American Revolution" and is home to more Revolutionary War sites than almost any other state. This book is so welcome because we do not celebrate our Bergen County historic sites enough. They are not only our heritage but should also be destinations for visitors just like the Jersey Shore and Atlantic City. Bergen County's imprint on American history is undeniable, with sites such as Historic New Bridge Landing, which contains the "bridge that saved the nation" and the Fort Lee Historic Park, which found its place in history in 1776 against the British. These Bergen County sites weave a tapestry of historic events that should be preserved for future generations.

I am pleased this book will celebrate Bergen County's rich legacy and enlighten the public at large as to the treasures that are right in their backyard.

—Loretta Weinberg, former New Jersey State Senator

FOREWORD

Bob Nesoff has a way with words…

And he takes you along on a journey through written words, you can actually feel that you are in that place and time.

In this book, Bob takes the reader back in time to visit some significant historical places in Bergen—New Jersey's most populous county. And you can tell that Bob enjoys every moment of it!

Through his descriptive and straightforward writing, Bob brings these historical locations alive and, by looking back, shows us how we moved ahead as a nation.

Enjoy the journey!

—John S. Hogan, County Clerk

1

NEW MILFORD

BIRTHPLACE OF BERGEN COUNTY

Sitting on the banks of the Hackensack River, the borough of New Milford is today a peaceful town that belies the history that lies within its borders ranging from well before the American Revolution and on into modern times. There are many homes dating to the 1600s, with some still in use today as private residences.

New Milford's location by the Hackensack River made it an easy destination from New York. The nearby Hudson River, critical to both sides in the War for Independence, was easily reached by boat from the East Bank. As real estate agents often say, "Look for location, location, location." New Milford had it all.

Arguably the first person to arrive and see the potential for what is now New Milford was French settler David Des Marest (also des Marets). The name morphed into Demarest, and many current county residents still bear the name. Others may be found as permanent residents of the numerous cemeteries that dot the county.

The island of Manhattan in New York, arguably the most expensive piece of real estate in the world today, is reputed to have been purchased from the Indians for a sum approximating twenty-four dollars in trade goods. If that be the case, New Milford was far more valuable.

According to a charter signed by David Demarest and Mendawasy, Sachem of the Tappan tribe, the Frenchman took title for

100 fathem of black wampum	15 fire lock guns
100 barrel of seed	one barrel of powder

100 fathem of white wampum	15 kettles
100 knives	4 barrels of beer
20 blankets	one saw
20 match coats	one anker of rum
20 hatchets	one pistol
20 shirt	30 pairs of stockings
1 carpenter awl	one plaine
20 hows [hoes]	One great knife

[Spellings are as listed on the 1677 bill of sale]

Although the total sum exceeded that of Manhattan's going price, it was still considered a great deal. The land was exceptionally fertile and arable for farming. The river at the base of the hill where Demarest built his home provided an ample water supply for crops. It was also navigable and had an abundant supply of fish. Wildlife abounded and provided a plentiful supply of fauna and fowl.

Over the early years, there was both peaceful interaction with the local Natives, the Leni Lenape, as well as periods of deadly conflict with both sides innocent and at fault. Settlers and Indians paid with their lives.

One of the earliest homes built in the town is known today as the Jacobus Demarest Homestead. The earliest portion of the building was constructed in 1677 by David Demarest Sr. and is considered to be the oldest home in the county. He was founder and leader of the French Huguenot colony in Bergen County. His grandson Jacobus was born in 1689 and lived in the house until his death in 1763. Jacobus's son, John, completed the house in 1765, and it remained in the Demarest family until 1850, when it was sold. Over the centuries, the home passed through several hands; today it is owned by the Casey family.

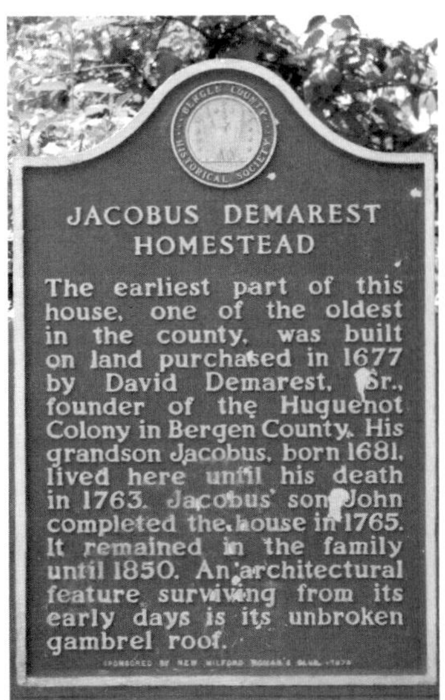

While a historic plaque placed at the edge of the property identifies it as the Jacobus Demarest Homestead, the Casey family, the most recent residents, tried to change the designation to the Demarest Casey Homestead, but that never came to pass. In a book on the history of New Milford, the house is listed as the Gurd-

Opposite: Plaque commemorating the Jacobus Demarest Homestead, oldest in New Milford (likely built in 1677, although some records claim 1765). The most recent occupants were the Casey family, until the death of Marlene Casey in 2020.

Above: The Jacobus Demarest Homestead shortly after the road in front was paved, a narrow passageway.

Casey House. There is no mention of Demarest, but that could be due to the fact that Alice Gurd Casey was on the committee preparing the book.

The house passed to Timothy Casey and his wife, Marlene. Tim passed away in the 1990s, and Marlene took sole ownership. She was active in a variety of historic activities and was a contributor to the creation of New Bridge Landing Historic site. She took up the cudgels to rename the home, but except in extraordinary circumstances, the building retains the name of the builder or first family to live there. She passed away in 2020, and the home was put on the market.

Marlene Casey truly enjoyed historical events. She would dress in period costume for historical activities and was known for working in her colonial-style kitchen, often canning her own fruits.

After the death of Jacobus Demarest in 1763, the home was kept in the family by Johannis Demarest, who lived there through the Revolution. His son, Casparus, followed him. The home was sold to the Zabriskie

The Jacobus Demarest Homestead, looking much in 2022 as it did more than 245 years ago.

family around 1850. They retained ownership until the early 1900s, when it was purchased by the Brookchester Land Company for use as an office. The Gurd/Caey family took ownership some years later and did major restoration work.

While New Milford's official designation is as a borough, it is commonly referred to as a "town." People have lived within its borders for more than three hundred years, far longer than any other town in Bergen County. Thus its designation as "The Birthplace of Bergen County."

FRENCH CEMETERY

The Huguenot Cemetery bears witness to the names of the early settlers. Today, the cemetery is fenced in as the result of some teen angst, as vandals knocked over the ancient headstones. But for those who would like to enter the grounds, the key may be obtained from police headquarters right across the road. While most of the stones are illegible from centuries of weather, some, such as several Demarests, can still be read and are a boon for those whose hobby is making copies of the inscriptions. The cemetery is the final

Left: Information sign at French Cemetery, burial ground for Revolutionary soldiers and New Milford's early settlers.

Below: Stones from early burials. Some can be read, but most letters have worn away over the centuries.

home for ten soldiers who served in the Revolution as well as one in the Civil War. One of the earliest interments is that of Cornelius Bogert, born in 1748 and buried in 1825. He served in the First Regiment of the Bergen County Militia.

Many of the names are familiar throughout the county as settlers moved on. There are Bogerts, Zabriskies and Demarests aplenty under the weathered stones.

Spaced out across the cemetery grounds are small white marker flags denoting locations where it is believed more of the original settlers have been laid to rest. Not far below and slightly to the west is the Hackensack River, once a major waterway for ships coming from Europe or just across the Hudson River in New York. Legend has it that as the Demarest family arrived at about this location, Marie Demarest, David's wife, lay dying in the ship, possibly of smallpox. She was taken ashore by her sons, who pleaded with the Lenni Lenape Indians (sometimes pronounced *Lena lenapee*. In the area, the more common pronunciation is *Lena len napee*) to permit her burial. Consent was given, and she lies somewhere in the Huguenot Cemetery. A small church was later built there and used for worship until it was moved to another location.

EARLY HOMES

On June 8, 1677, Demarest purchased the land from the tribe for wampum, coats, pants, weapons, powder for the guns and other trade goods. Included were items later banned for trade with the Natives: several barrels of beer and an "anker of rum." This sum was considerably more than settlers paid for the purchase of the area of Newark, New Jersey's biggest city. Newark was originally named "Milford," and an unsubstantiated legend dictates that the borough derived its name from that city.

In New Milford, Lawrence Van Buskirk acquired some 1,076 acres of land just south of New Bridge Road on the current southern border of the town. It was adjacent to land owned by the Demarests. That started a long series of intermarriages between the two families.

In 1678, David Demarest built a home that now stands at Historic New Bridge Landing in the adjacent town of River Edge. The aforementioned Demarest Homestead, built in 1677, is arguably the oldest house in town today. It stands on River Road at the intersection of River Edge Avenue and is difficult to see due to the tall phalanx of shrubs.

Natoli's General Store in New Milford. Note the horse-drawn wagon, probably late 1800s or early 1900s.

A canoe plies a tree-covered and pristine Hackensack River between New Milford and River Edge, a far cry from what it is today.

Today New Milford boasts about fifteen homes that date back to the origins of our country's history. The book *The Story of New Milford, Birthplace of Bergen County*, a great source of information for us, notes that "New Milford is far from being a Williamsburg or Old Sturbridge." It nonetheless treasures and preserves its history. The book, published in 1964, is currently out of print, and only a few copies survive.

Some of the other "ancient" homes still standing include:

The Bloomer-Hart House, 147 River Edge Avenue, located at Old Bridge. Built about 1840 by George Demarest, it contains a wing that may date back to 1790 but could actually be decades older. The front is constructed of brick with sides of red Jersey sandstone, indicating the builder was rather well-to-do—brick fronts were considered a status symbol. Interestingly, the brook that now flows nearby was once directed to flow through the home's basement to provide a continuous supply of fresh water and held a pen for live fish.

The Walter-Campbell House, 715 River Road, appears on a Revolutionary War map with annotation that it belonged to Jacob Campbell. It is estimated to have been built in 1774.

Trautwein House, 175 Boulevard, is shown on a map in 1861 as belonging to J.D. Demarest. It is a small building that may have originally been an outbuilding. Located near the brook, it may have been a springhouse. In a dark part of history, there is suspicion that it may have been a slave house or farm building.

2

TAPPAN

OLD '76 HOUSE

Tappan's Old '76 House could claim the title of being one of the oldest taverns in the New Jersey/New York corridor, but few can dispute the fact that it was the location for events that could have altered the Revolution and had us all pledging allegiance to Queen Elizabeth.

And it has the ghosts to prove it.

The tavern sits today on the dividing line between Bergen County in New Jersey and Rockland County, New York. The ancient eatery's parking lot is situated in Bergen County, while the tavern itself resides in New York. The entire tract was part of Bergen County until the two states established a dividing line that split the property between the two states.

Today it not only serves fine modern food but also boasts the ghosts of a woman, a man and two children of undetermined origin that have served as an exciting addition to a peaceful meal. Robb Norden, who has owned the establishment for thirty-five years, has seen the spectral figures, as have any number of people there for a meal. One, a woman, appears at a window table in the south end of the dining room, while a male visits diners at the opposite end.

Speculation is that the male ghost seen at a corner table might be that of infamous British spy Major John André, hanged on the hill behind the tavern. The ghost visits the '76 frequently but gives no clue about who he actually is, what he is looking for or what he wants. He simply appears, moves around the west end of the dining room and then goes back to wherever ghosts go.

Marker outside the Old '76 House in Tappan, New York, where British spy John André was confined before his execution.

He doesn't speak and makes no attempt to have contact with staff or diners. But some of those who have actually seen him describe a man in civilian clothes typical of the late 1700s. Major André was convicted of spying because he wore such clothes rather than a uniform.

"The only ones that bother me," commented Norden, "are the two children. They only appear on the second floor. Seeing, as I have, the ghosts of two young children, a boy and girl, is bothersome. I don't know who they are or what their story is." But, Norden says, the fact that two children died so young is bothersome.

But there is proof. Norden produced a photo that has a spectral being in it. "A young couple had their wedding reception here some time back. After they left I received a call from the bride asking me who the lady in a blue dress was that photo-bombed a picture. When I saw the photo, it took me aback. It was the female ghost who was the uninvited guest at the reception."

Although it's known as the Old '76 House, the tavern was first built in 1686 by Caspares Mabie as a home and tavern. Mabie was a local merchant turned innkeeper, and the tavern was known originally as Mabie's Inn.

The tavern ended up as part of Rockland County, New York, just a musket ball's flight from the border. While many people think of Lower Manhattan's Fraunces Tavern as being the oldest in the area (it was the site of Washington's farewell to his officers following the end of the Revolutionary War), it went through several iterations from its opening in 1762. Fraunces was named Sign of Queen Charlotte and then Queen's Head Tavern. It ceased operations for a while and then reopened as a tavern in 1783 by Samuel Fraunces.

The Old '76 House lays claim to have been built in 1668. During and before the Revolution, the tavern was host to Patriots planning the separation from England. It was considered a safe ground and meeting place for the revolutionaries. It came into everlasting prominence following the most notorious act of deceit and infamy in American history: the calumny of Benedict Arnold.

General Arnold had been posted to command of the fort at West Point, a strategic position atop the Palisades overlooking the Hudson River.

The Old '76 House is said to be haunted. This is an unretouched image of what appears to be the female ghost photo-bombing a couple at lunch.

Entrance to the Old '76 House, looking as it did in the 1600s.

Should a British fleet manage to move beyond that point, it could have meant disaster for the nascent revolution. Embittered because he felt he had been downplayed and not given the high honors and position he felt he deserved, Arnold conspired with the British command to turn over the plans for the defense of Fort West Point. Add to that the fact the Congress had subjected him to a courts-martial. The Continental Congress owed Arnold money and delayed payment or refused to pay. He took matters into his own hands and pocketed funds at his disposal to make up for the debt. Congress took a dim view, charged him with misappropriating funds and put him on trial. It was too much for his oversized ego. Arnold contacted British officers and began his betrayal.

Arnold's contact was a young British officer, Major John André. André was considered a charming and handsome young man and was adjutant general to General Sir Henry Clinton, commander-in-chief of British forces in North America. Arnold was a brilliant and respected general and a close friend of Washington. But he had been reprimanded by Congress and even made to stand before a court-martial.

Arnold met with André and gave him drawings of the fortifications and other pertinent information that would have led to the collapse of the American strong point. The British officer mounted his horse and made his way through the lines. His movement raised the suspicions of several American troops, and they stopped and searched him. In his boot were the plans for West Point's defense. He was to have been taken by rowboat to a British sloop on the Hudson but was convinced that was too dangerous and he should leave on horseback. That was a fatal error. The plan had been for Arnold to replace a link on the huge chain spanning the Hudson River to prevent enemy ships from making it upstream. (One of those links today is displayed at West Point.) The link would be replaced by rope while the one taken was alleged to be repaired. Had the plot succeeded, British warships would have easily breeched the rope, breaking the chain, and enabling them to move forces upriver and capture Albany and major portions of upstate New York.

André was taken to the tavern, now the Old '76 House, then called Mabie's Inn, following his trial at the Old Dutch Church, a block away. He had been apprehended in civilian clothing and, as a result, was tried, convicted of spying and sentenced to hang.

Oddly, there were several Americans who attempted to intervene on his behalf with George Washington, but the American commander refused to step in. Had André been wearing a uniform, he would have been detained as an enemy soldier. In civilian clothes, he was a spy, and the penalty was death

Old Dutch Church, directly across from the Old '76 House. André was tried and convicted here. The bodies of Baylor's Dragoons (see section on River Vale) are buried in front of the church after being brought from the tanning vat.

by hanging. André requested to be executed by firing squad, as befitted his position. Hanging was for common criminals and lower caste people. Washington denied the request, and the major was hanged near the '76 House. A local woman threw a handful of peach pits into the shallow grave in a sign of disparagement to the spy.

Today several documents written and signed by André hang on the walls of the Old '76 House.

Much like Nathan Hale's last words, "I regret that I have but one life to give for my country," André is reputed to have said, "All I request, gentlemen, is that while I acknowledge the propriety of my sentence, you will bear me witness that I die like a brave man."

So taken by the young officer, Washington commented, "He was more unfortunate than criminal: An accomplished and gallant officer." An amazing tribute to an enemy soldier. Today André is a hero in England and respected in the United States. Arnold was disrespected on both sides of the Atlantic and died a despised man. Today, Washington's words are inscribed on the rear of the monument at the site of André's execution.

George Washington used the tavern for his headquarters while in the area, and many of the Continentals' battle plans were drawn up there. One

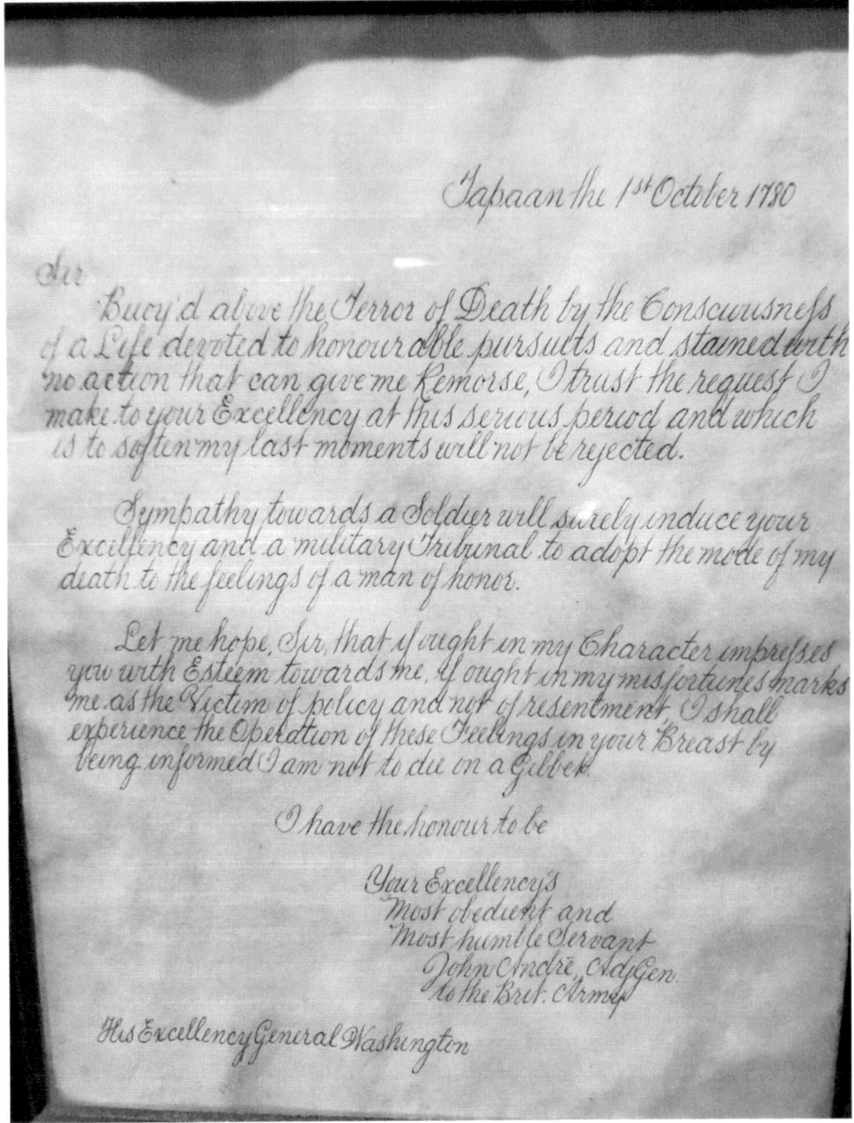

Tapaan the 1st October 1780

Sir

Buoy'd above the Terror of Death by the Consciousness of a Life devoted to honourable pursuits and stained with no action that can give me Remorse, I trust the request I make to your Excellency at this serious period and which is to soften my last moments will not be rejected.

Sympathy towards a Soldier will surely induce your Excellency and a military Tribunal to adopt the mode of my death to the feelings of a man of honor.

Let me hope, Sir, that if ought in my Character impresses you with Esteem towards me, if ought in my misfortunes marks me as the Victim of policy and not of resentment, I shall experience the Operation of these Feelings in your Breast by being informed I am not to die on a Gibbet.

I have the honour to be

Your Excellency's
Most obedient and
Most humble Servant
John André, Adj Gen.
to the Brit. Army

His Excellency General Washington

Above: One of a collection of original letters handwritten by Major André that adorn a wall in the tavern.

Opposite, left: Stone marker on actual site of Major André's execution by hanging. The words, though faded, are kind to him and note that he was mourned by both British and Americans.

Opposite, right: Reverse of stone marker with an inscription by George Washington, saying that André was "more unfortunate than criminal: He was an accomplished man and a gallant officer."

day while Washington was at lunch, he looked up and saw a picture of his former friend turned traitor Benedict Arnold hanging over the fireplace. Incensed, Washington rose, went to the fireplace and turned the drawing upside-down. It remains in the position to this day.

In 1880, André's body was exhumed for reburial in Westminster Abbey in London. The peach pits had taken their toll and grown into a peach tree. The tree's roots encircled the British spy's head and had to be trimmed so the remains could be removed. Today, rightfully considered a hero by the British, he lies in a separate section of Westminster Abbey, where access is limited. A stone monument today marks the spot where André was hanged and his nearby burial spot. The monument has been damaged over the years by vandals who, in all probability, objected to any honor for a foreign spy. André, in England, is regarded as a hero, while Benedict Arnold was reviled and shunned by both friend and foe. His name today stands for treachery. While the tavern was never in actuality a prison, it was referred to locally for many years to come as "André Prison." He was, in fact, held there before his trial and while awaiting execution.

For centuries, the tavern was host to travelers and served as host to ordinary folk and legends such as Washington himself. Virtually every Continental army general of the "West Wing" division dined in the establishment. It was also a safe haven for Patriots of the nascent nation to meet as they developed plans to fight the redcoats on their way to independence.

George Washington was at lunch in the Old '76 House when he spotted a picture of Benedict Arnold above the fireplace. He quietly walked over and turned the picture upside-down. It remains that way today.

In the eighteenth century, taverns were often centers of social life, and that held true for the '76 House. After the plotting of the Revolution, it became a place where local news was shared and business discussed. It was central for celebrations, weddings and receptions following the burial of a local citizen.

Over the years, as with many historic buildings, maintenance became a major problem. It offered a challenge to restore and maintain its history. Modern construction requirements obviously did not exist. Think of the leaning Tower of Pisa. The Old '76 House had similar problems. The original stone foundation was not properly laid or supported and failed to settle uniformly. Much of the original floor and ceiling joists had structural problems as a result of the way in which the foundation settled. They were braced with modern materials inconsistent with the historic building.

The original floor plan and layout of the interior of the building reconfigured many of the rooms. There was even a totally false "André's Prison" room designed to lure visitors to a historic site. Those restoring the building were tasked with locating the original plans and documents detailing the building as it was designed. They then had to translate the restoration design in a sound manner. Staying true to history, the André Room has been relegated to the dustbin of false history.

The work was made easier by the history of the building. There were readily available accounts of the Old '76 House's interior as a result of the frequent meetings and other events held there. These detailed the interior spaces, what they were used for, the original design and what changes took place over the centuries. The preservationists discovered that the building was constructed in three phases. In the first, there were two rooms and a small second level. The following phase was undertaken several years before André came into the picture. It held what is today's bar and dining area, where the British spy was actually held.

Finally, the last effort was undertaken in the past century. Architect J. Alberto Robaina went to work putting together a design that incorporated the original in a favorable design along with updated requirements. The first step was to work on the foundation, which had withstood three centuries but was both outdated and in serious need of work. Footings were dug by hand with some thirty tons of clay and dirt removed and replaced by poured concrete. Once a solid foundation was set, the next job was locating interior lumber consistent with the original.

Looking for ceiling joists, they finally located a barn in Ontario, Canada, that was actually older than the '76 House. Continuing with the architectural investigation with an eye toward keeping the project historically correct, the crew located so-called nondimensional red pine flooring in an Amish schoolhouse near Lancaster, Pennsylvania. The next step brought them to Europe and Holland, famed for its Delft tile work. There they had tiles hand-painted and brought the finished product back to Tappan, where they were set in place in the Tap Room.

In the original construction, the preferred method of mixing plaster was to use a combination of horsehair. Rather than remove the ancient material, the workers retouched plaster in the four original rooms of the tavern. Since electricity was still to be invented and was not in the original construction, wiring and air conditioning ducts had to be installed without any damage to the three-hundred-year-old atmosphere. The ductwork was hidden under custom molded wainscoting. Finishing materials were chosen and applied from colonial palettes supplied by some of the top preservation-oriented firms.

It took more than a decade of finely detailed work, including research and the combination of the old with modern construction requirements to make a modern '76 House look the way it was when General George Washington

Tavern owner Rob Norden, behind the bar, hefts an ancient flintlock gun, part of his Revolutionary-era collection on display in the Old '76 House.

dined there and British hero and spy Major John André walked through its doors. Some to fame, others to infamy.

Today, the Old '76 House welcomes diners and visitors who enjoy fine food and a sense of history.

Sitting within the hallowed walls of the tavern, you can feel the history and, if you try hard enough, see the spirits of the founding fathers meeting there to plot independence. And that might not be just your imagination. In 2012, a group of paranormal investigators looked into alleged happenings there. Their decision was that spirits inhabit the Old '76 House. Could it be Major André seeking redemption? Could it be George Washington planning to meet with his officers to discuss coming battle plans? Is that man in colonial garb and white wig a reenactor or a spirit of the past? If you are adventurous, request a seat at table no. 2. That's where most paranormal incidents are alleged to have taken place. Try placing an order for yourself and your guests—and whomever else might suddenly appear. You decide.

Old '76 House
110 Main Street
Tappan, NY 10983
845-359-5476
https://76House.com/

3

BERGEN COUNTY HISTORY

AN OVERVIEW

DIVERSITY FROM THE BEGINNING UNTIL TODAY

From the days of its earliest settlers, sans the original occupants and their various tribes, Bergen County has always been a model melting pot of nationalities, religions and cultures. And while there was a proliferation of differences, they did not always mesh well. The earliest European settlers were from Holland, followed by English and a smattering of French, German and whomever else found their way onto a ship for the brutal monthslong trans-Atlantic crossing in a leaky wooden sailing ship. Many made the crossing. Others only got off the ship when their bodies were encased in canvas bags and consigned to the sea.

Through it all—harsh winters, ethnic conflicts and revolution—they managed to hang on and build a society that, today, offers diversity seen in few other places, with the possible exception of neighboring New York City. There are descendants of the original settlers still inhabiting the county. There are relative newcomers: escaped and freed slaves, those in bondage for European debts and so many more.

Much of the diversity, while alive and well in suburban towns, is seen primarily in cities such as Paterson, Union City, Newark, Clifton, Trenton and more. In Bergen County, the melding is seen in such towns as Teaneck, where at one time the mayor, Mohammed Hameeddudin, a Muslim, served alongside his close friend and deputy mayor Elie Y. Katz, an Orthodox Jew.

As noted in numerous places throughout this book, the Lenape people were in residence. Their subtribes included the Tappan, Hackensack, Munsee and Rumachenanck, who were later called the Haverstraw.

A group called the Ramapough Mountain Indians, with clusters in Mahwah and other counties, fought for designation as a tribe. Although there was considerable debate and opposition to such a designation, it was conferred by the state in 1980. Much of the opposition came from those who felt there never was such a tribe. In fact, the so-called tribe was a conglomeration of ethnicities: Native Americans, those who escaped slavery, Hessian soldiers who remained in the colonies, White trappers and others. The Ramapough were colloquially referred to as "Jackson Whites." The reference was to "Jacks," a derogatory name for Black men and the "Whites" for the Hessians, traders and others who found their way atop the mountain.

In fact, over the years their home atop Stag Hill in Mahwah became a closed society to the extent that few outsiders were permitted access. There were rumors of people, hunters and curiosity seekers who ventured onto the mountain and disappeared. Most of these stories were untrue, but the mystique persisted, fueled by the residents themselves.

A reporter for the county daily newspaper assigned to do a feature on the community was warned by a resident, a Mr. Mann. The name was common on the hill as a result of years of inbreeding, marrying among the small population of mountain residents. Mann told the reporter that he had best leave: "If the others find out you are a reporter fella, there would be a problem."

Those in recent history who would venture to the top of Stag Hill along an unpaved road would notice a cutoff with a parked car and a driver simply sitting there. Under normal circumstances, visitors were not stopped or interfered with. However, if the visitor caused a problem, he would find the way down blocked by the car in the cutoff.

Today, Stag Hill is much like any other suburban subdivision. The road is paved, there is no "security guard" at the cutoff and there are no more rumors about people disappearing. Homes are neat and appealing, and with the magnificent view from the top, it is a beautiful and quiet neighborhood.

Early efforts by Dutch settlers in the mid-1600s were not met with approbation by the Native Americans, and conflict took place. The European attempts to settle the region were forced back to the western shore of the Hudson River and formed Bergen Township, the first permanent European settlement in the area.

In the second of what came to be known as the Dutch-Anglo Wars, New York governor Peter Stuyvesant capitulated to the British navy and the English took control. The Province of New Jersey passed an act in 1675 creating Bergen County. In 1683, Bergen, as one of four of the original counties, was recognized as an independent county by the provincial assembly.

During the Revolution, Bergen was the focal point of several pivotal battles with the British. The Continentals were forced from the strategic position in Fort Lee across the Hudson from Fort Washington in 1776 and made their way through Englewood, Teaneck and Bergenfield, crossing the Hackensack River at New Bridge, one of the few river crossings. The Patriots destroyed the bridge to hinder the oncoming Brits intent on capturing George Washington. A new bridge today stands at the site of the destroyed bridge at New Bridge Landing Historic Park (see page 157 for more).

The British rained terror on the Continentals, as evidenced by the Baylor Massacre (see page 165). Patriot dragoons were asleep in a barn owned by a Tory who informed the British that they were there. The Loyalist troops attacked while the Americans were asleep, bayonetting many of them and shooting the others. As described later in this book, they were buried in a tanning vat along a river in what today is the Borough of River Vale.

Over the years, Bergen County was parceled out to form other political jurisdictions. Portions went to New York State, forming Tappan, while others formed towns in Hudson and Passaic Counties.

In 1894, the state legislature passed legislation permitting counties to create municipalities, and Bergen took that to the extreme. Today, there are seventy individual and sovereign municipalities, each with its own local government.

The George Washington Bridge was built in 1931, connecting Fort Lee to Manhattan and opening a flurry of building in Bergen County. The population exploded.

In 1955, during the height of the Cold War, the U.S. Army built a missile base at Campgaw Mountain to fend off any Russian attack. The attack never came, the base was decommissioned and today it is part of the county park system, hosting a horse stable.

The first census available was taken in 1790 and showed Bergen with a population of 12,601. From 1900 (78,441) to the next census in 1910 (138,002), growth was exponential. In 1940, the first census after the George Washington Bridge opened, the county boasted 409,646 residents. The growth was steady after that until the 2019 estimate of 932,202 made Bergen the most populous county in the state.

The county is home to a wide range of economic spheres, from predominantly blue collar in the south to upscale in the north. Alpine, along Route 9W, is home to such personalities as former Yankee pitcher and future Hall of Famer C.C. Sabathia and comedian and actor Eddie Murphy. Alpine, Saddle River and other towns are frequent inclusions when lists of the wealthiest towns in the country are named.

George Washington and his fellow Patriots could never have imagined what their blood and sweat would create. Enjoy Bergen County. You can hardly take a step or drive through its streets without passing a historic cemetery or a building from its earliest days that is still in use as a residence. Enjoy the trip.

4

CELEBRITIES BURIED IN BERGEN COUNTY

As might be expected, in an area predating the American Revolution, such as Bergen County, there are a host of notables buried within its borders. For instance, there is the Gethsemane Cemetery, located on Liberty Street just off Route 46 West in Little Ferry.

Gethsemane contains less than an acre and has some five hundred African Americans buried therein. Today, there are fewer than fifty gravestones still intact. In 1994, the cemetery was listed to the National Register of Historic Places (NRHP).

One of the notables buried here is Elizabeth Sutliff Duffer (d. 1880). She was a former slave who overcame her background and became the owner of the second-largest clay company in the state. Two others are Civil War veterans who were among the Black soldiers fighting on the side of the Union. They were Peter Billings and Silas Carpenter.

As Bergen County grew, and with its convenient location a stone's throw to the west of New York City, it became home to a host of notables and celebrities who were then buried in a variety of cemeteries. Most of the burial grounds are open to the public, but it always pays to check in advance and make sure the gates haven't been closed.

The nirvana of celebrity cemeteries is, of course, Père Lachaise Cemetery in Paris, which holds the likes of Jim Morrison, leader of the musical group the Doors. He is joined by expatriate writer Gertrude Stein and her longtime companion and lover, Alice B. Toklas. Visitors, primarily American, wear a rut in the cemetery's roadway leading to Morrison's grave, the most visited there.

Graves of John Marley and his wife, Syd, in Cedar Park Cemetery in Paramus. In a famous scene from the movie *Godfather*, Marley's character awakens to find a severed horse's head in his bloody bed.

While Bergen County cannot compete with Jim Morrison or his resting place, it doesn't lack for big names spending eternity here.

Musician Jeff Hyman is at rest in Hillside Cemetery in Lyndhurst. Jeff who? You might better know him as Joey Ramone of The Ramones. His stone is an oversized headstone listing him as "Loving Son and Brother A.K.A Joey Ramone. Rock and Roll Hall of Famer." Jeff was born on May 19, 1951, and moved into Hillside on April 15, 2001.

Traditionally, those visiting graves of Jewish decedents leave a small stone atop graves to mark their visit. Acolytes visiting Hyman leave sunglasses, guitar picks, charms and other memorabilia.

Make him an offer he can't refuse? Have him wake up to a horse's head in his bloody bed? Actor John Marley, who played the intimidated producer in the first *Godfather* film, is in permanent residence in Paramus's Cedar Park Cemetery, a major Jewish cemetery covering acres of ground.

No, there is no depiction of any part of a horse on his grave marker.

Author and Nobel laureate Isaac Bashevis Singer is a neighbor of John Marley, but he rests in the Beth-El section of the cemetery. Singer was born in Poland and later came to the United States. He first gained fame writing

Top and middle: Grave markers for Isaac Bashevis Singer, Nobel laureate and famous author. He is buried in Beth-El Cemetery, adjacent to Cedar Park.

Bottom: Marker for Sandy Nesoff, prominent New Jerseyan, involved in numerous charitable works and co-founder of a prestigious national journalism association.

in Yiddish and later in English. Singer wrote about Holocaust survivors and the displaced people of Europe.

Also located in the Beth-El section only yards from Singer is Sandy Nesoff, a prominent resident of Bergen County, listed in Who's Who in America and Who's Who in New Jersey. A history aficionado, she was instrumental in preserving the story of New Milford. A time capsule buried in front of the municipal building was one of her main projects to tell the story of the town to another generation. It was buried for twenty-five years and opened in early spring of 2022. All the artifacts were well preserved and are on display in the town's municipal building. She was well known in the political sector of the county for her activities until her passing in 2021. Prior to her passing, she was assisting in the preparation and research for this book.

And while we are discussing movies, Alice Guy-Blaché, who broke through the testosterone wall in filmmaking and became the first woman to own a movie studio, is buried in Maryrest Cemetery, a Roman Catholic cemetery, in Mahwah. Her studio was also a Bergen County landmark, located in Fort Lee, birthplace of modern movies.

Maryrest is located across from Campgaw Mountain County Park and down the road from the county's police and fire academy. It is also right by the Rio Vista enclave on Seminary Road, an up-up-upscale development of multimillion-dollar homes that deserves a drive-by just to see what's there.

Obviously, the arts are well represented below ground in Bergen County. Salsa legend Frankie Ruiz is forever at rest in the borough of Fair Lawn at Fair Lawn Memorial Cemetery. Not far off in the county seat of Hackensack, Ben E. King may be horizontal, but will be forever remembered for his Drifters version of "Stand by Me." He is in repose in the Hackensack Cemetery on River Road.

Minutes away in Paramus's George Washington Memorial Park is the musician King replaced as front man for the Drifters, Clyde McPhatter.

Famed poet and physician William Carlos Williams is in repose in Lyndhurst's Hillsdale Cemetery.

While making rubbings of gravestones to bring home a souvenir has been a popular pastime when visiting celebrities at rest, cemetery officials discourage the act. Most rubbings are made with paper placed over the inscription, and then the face is rubbed with soft pencil, charcoal or some other substance that will produce a true image of the face of the stone. Officials fear that continued use of the practice will ultimately damage the stones, especially the old and fragile ones dating back centuries.

Many cemeteries provide maps showing where individuals are buried, while others do not. You might try speaking with an employee in the field, as they often know the address of virtually every resident. Or, before going, check out the website findagrave.com. That could make life easier for the living.

Now go. Enjoy the dead.

5

BERGEN COUNTY HISTORIC SITES

Note: While many of these sites are written about in detail within the pages of this book, the writers felt it important to provide a comprehensive listing of historical sites in Bergen County. To write about all of them would have required a book considerably larger than this one.

Aviation Hall of Fame & Museum of New Jersey
400 Fred Wehran Drive
Teterboro, NJ 07608

Founded in 1972, the NJAHOF exists to showcase New Jersey's 214-year contribution to the history of human flight. In addition to the Hall of Fame, which recognizes those who have made outstanding aeronautical achievements that have brought worldwide recognition to the state, the museum contains a number of unique exhibits: the rocket engine that propelled the X-15 to incredible speed and height records; the first American hovercraft, invented by Charles Fletcher; helicopters; a newly restored OV1 Grumman Mohawk; many airplane models; and other exhibits. The museum holds public events throughout the year, including the Wings & Wheels Expos.

Baylor Massacre Burial Site
County Historic Site
Rivervale Road and Red Oak Drive
River Vale, NJ 07675

This Bergen County–owned wooded park contained the burial site of the Third Continental Light Dragoons who, on September 28, 1778, were slain during the notorious Revolutionary War event known today as the Baylor Massacre. The original burial site on the banks of the Hackensack River is now marked with the site's original millstone. The remains were discovered during an archaeological survey in 1967. They now rest in the graveyard of the Old Dutch Reformed Church in Tappan, New York. This historic park contains accessible pathways and historic interpretive panels describing the history of the Baylor Massacre. Open during daylight hours.

Bergen County Court House
10 Main Street
Hackensack, NJ 07601

The Bergen County Court House, located in the historic heart of the county on the Hackensack River, was designed by James Riely Gordon (1863–1937), the prominent architect responsible for the design of about seventy courthouses and two state capitols. The cornerstone was laid on July 6, 1910, and the courthouse was completed in 1912. Designed in the Beaux-Arts style, reflecting monuments of classical Rome and Italian Renaissance, the courthouse incorporated rich materials, including marble and bronze. The dome was modeled on the U.S. Capitol dome

Bishop House
(Ackerman-Dewsnap House)
176 East Saddle River Road
Saddle River, NJ 07458

The Ackerman-Dewsnap Home, which is more popularly known as the Bishop House, was built around 1835 by the Ackerman family. Located in the Saddle River Valley, this house was first added onto by owner James Dewsnap around 1870. It was renovated following World War II when the Bishop family acquired the property. It now serves as the community's cultural center and is in the National Register of Historic Places.

Cadmus House

14-01 Pollitt Drive
Fair Lawn, NJ 07410

The Cadmus House, the official museum for the Borough of Fair Lawn, is a Dutch sandstone building located on Pollitt Drive next to the Radburn railroad station. The museum has historical artifacts of Fair Lawn ranging from Native American arrowheads to Word War I and II uniforms; maps from the 1880s; old farm tools and parts of the former Hopper-Croucher farmhouse. Upstairs are the Victorian Room with period furniture and toys and the Fireman's Room displaying old firefighting equipment and pictures of early firefighters and the 1941 Plaza Building fire.

Camp Merritt Memorial Monument

County Historic Site
Knickerbocker Road and Madison Avenue
Cresskill, NJ 07626

Camp Merritt Memorial Monument marks the center of an important World War I embarkation camp, where more than 1 million U.S. soldiers passed through on their way to and from the battlefields of Europe. In August 1919, the Bergen County Freeholders purchased land for the monument at what was the approximate center of the camp. Modeled on the Washington Monument, the memorial is a sixty-five-foot-high granite obelisk. On the base are the names of the 578 people who died in the camp, mostly as a result of the 1918 worldwide influenza epidemic. A large Art Deco–style carved relief by the sculptor Robert Ingersoll Aitken (1878–1949) shows a striding "doughboy" with an eagle flying overhead. In the ground is a three-dimensional stone carving of the map of the 770-acre Camp Merritt. The monument was dedicated on May 30, 1924. General John J. "Black Jack" Pershing gave the dedicatory address to a crowd of 20,000 people.

Carlstadt Firehouse Museum
Division Avenue and Sixth Street
Carlstadt, NJ 07072

The museum, run by the Carlstadt Historical Society, houses a remarkable collection that includes archival photographs, written documents, news articles, clothing and other items that bring the borough's colorful history to life. You can find everything from 1930s school pennants and early twentieth-century fife and drum corps uniforms to a vintage breathalyzer used by the police department.

The Civil War Drill Hall Theatre
130 Grand Avenue
Leonia, NJ 07605

Home of the Players Guild of Leonia (PGL), this building was constructed about 1859 and is the last extant structure in Bergen County with direct links to the Civil War. In the years leading up to the Civil War, it served as headquarters and training center for Company K of the Twenty-Second Regiment of Volunteer Infantry, the only regiment recruited entirely within the county to serve in the Civil War. The PGL is a community theater group founded in 1919 and offers musicals, comedies, classic and contemporary dramas, children's theater and special events throughout the year.

Easton Tower
County Historic Site
Red Mill Road, Route 4 and Saddle River Road
Paramus, NJ 07652

Easton Tower is a unique site in Bergen County. This picturesque stone and wood frame structure located in the Arcola section of Paramus was built in 1899 on the original George Easton estate along the Saddle River as part of a spacious landscaped water park. Surrounded by busy roadways, it is now adjacent to and accessible by the Saddle River Bikeway.

The Fell House
475 Franklin Turnpike
Allendale, NJ 07401

Originally called Peterfield, this mid-eighteenth-century mansion was the home of John Fell, Bergen County Revolutionary War Patriot and member of the First Continental Congress of the United States. Fell was a merchant who before the Revolution had vessels plying the Hackensack and Passaic Rivers. He served the county as a justice of the peace and a judge of the Court of Common Pleas. As a member of the First Continental Congress of the United States, Fell ratified the Constitution. During the Revolution, he had a reputation as a great Tory hunter, and on April 22, 1777, Fell was taken prisoner at his home by a band of twenty-five Loyalist raiders and imprisoned in New York City. Fell was paroled on January 7, 1778, and permitted to go home on May 11. Fell kept a diary while he was a member of the Congress for the State of New Jersey from November 6, 1778, to November 30, 1779. The original is kept in the Library of Congress. Open for special events.

Fort Lee Historic Park
(Palisades Interstate Park)
Hudson Terrace
Fort Lee, NJ 07024

Located on the cliffs overlooking the Hudson River with spectacular views of the George Washington Bridge, Fort Lee played a significant part in America's fight for independence when General Washington and his Continental army, stationed here, were driven out by the advancing British army in November 1776. It was the beginning of New Jersey's role as the Crossroads of the American Revolution. The visitor center provides information on the role of Fort Lee in the American Revolution with two floors of displays that tell the story of the tumultuous New York campaign of the fall of 1776—culminating in the Continental army's "Retreat to Victory" across the Jerseys. Events are held here throughout the year, and visitors can walk the paths and enjoy the scenic views of the Hudson River.

Fort Lee Museum at the Judge Moore House
1588 Palisade Avenue
Fort Lee, NJ 07024

The historic 1922 Judge Moore House, home of the Fort Lee Museum, was built out of native bluestone and is one of the state's most architecturally significant buildings located in a particularly scenic area of downtown Fort Lee. It contains historical exhibits and displays of documents, photographs and artifacts from Fort Lee's past, including material from the famed Riviera Nightclub, the George Washington Bridge and the American Revolution.

Garretson Forge and Farm
County Historic Site
4-02 River Road
Fair Lawn, NJ 07410

Garretson Farm, near the Passaic River in Fair Lawn, is one of the oldest Dutch homesteads in Bergen County. The sandstone house and farm were occupied by six generations of the Garretson family, from 1720 through the middle of the twentieth century. It is the headquarters of the Garretson Forge and Farm Society, which holds events here throughout the year. Growing in the site's extensive heirloom gardens, which are maintained by the Master Gardeners of Bergen County and Society volunteers, are over fifty varieties of medicinal and culinary herbs and a pantry garden. The farmstead is also a certified Monarch Butterfly Way Station.

Gethsemane Cemetery
County Historic Site
Summit Place off Route 46
Little Ferry, NJ 07643

Gethsemane Cemetery is a county-owned historic African American cemetery located west of the Hackensack River in Little Ferry. It was established in 1860 as the burial ground for the "colored population" of the village of Hackensack. This historic cemetery was added to the State and National Registers of Historic Places for the significant role it played in the enactment of New Jersey's early civil rights legislation as well as containing evidence of West African burial customs. The one-acre site contains four meditation areas with historic interpretive panels. Three panels list the names of over five hundred people buried here. Open by appointment only; school groups are welcome. Free.

The Hermitage Museum
335 North Franklin Turnpike
Ho-Ho-Kus, NJ 07423

This National Historic Landmark started out as a circa 1760 Dutch sandstone house that was visited during the Revolutionary War by General George Washington. It was also the site of the marriage of Aaron Burr and Theodosia Prevost. It was remodeled in 1847 by noted architect William H. Ranlett and is an outstanding example of the romantic Gothic Revival style of architecture. Educational programs for all ages, lectures and special events are held year-round. The Hermitage is open to the public for guided tours year-round Wednesday through Sunday.

Hiram Blauvelt Art Museum
705 Kinderkamack Road
Oradell, NJ 07649

The Hiram Blauvelt Art Museum is located high on a hill in the historic 1893 cedar shingle and turret-style building that was the original carriage house of the Blauvelt Estate. The museum was established in 1957 and features the work of contemporary wildlife artists.

Historic New Bridge Landing
Campbell-Christie House
Demarest and Steuben House
1201–9 Main Street
River Edge, NJ 07661

Elevated to the ranks of New Jersey's newest state park in October 2004, Historic New Bridge Landing contains three New Jersey Dutch stone houses: the 1752 Steuben House, a state historic site; the 1774 Campbell-Christie House, a Bergen County Historic Site; and the late-eighteenth century Demarest House, owned by the Blauvelt Demarest Foundation. All are furnished with period furnishings. The site also contains the 1889 Pratt-type low truss swing bridge at the site crossing the Hackensack River of the original eighteenth-century "Bridge That Saved the Nation"; the 1889 Westervelt Barn; and a reproduction eighteenth-century out kitchen. The Steuben House is an esteemed Revolutionary War landmark. It was built at a strategic river crossing, which served as an encampment, battleground, military headquarters and intelligence-gathering post. The Campbell-Christie House serves as the headquarters of the Bergen County Historical Society, which regularly holds events on this site.

Hopper-Goetschius House Museum
245 Lake Street
Upper Saddle River, NJ 07458

The Hopper-Goetschius house on the corner of Lake Street and East Saddle River Road dates back to 1739. Built by the Hopper family, it is the oldest remaining house in Upper Saddle River. In 1814, the house became the home of the Reverend Stephen Goetschius and remained in the family for over 150 years. This site also contains the Van Riper–Tice New World Dutch Barn, which was moved here in 1989 to save it from demolition. The site now serves as the headquarters of the Upper Saddle River Historical Society, which regularly holds events and gives tours of the buildings.

James Rose Center

506 East Ridgewood Avenue
Ridgewood, NJ 07451

This was the home of James Rose, one of the twentieth century's leaders of the modern movement in American landscape architecture. His home served as a constantly changing laboratory for his residential landscape designs. The house and grounds are open to the public for self-guided tours May through September. The mission of the James Rose Center is to promote sound environmental design through public lectures, student internships, awards, public outreach, preservation and research. Group tours are available by appointment.

Kearney House

Palisades Interstate Park
Alpine Approach Road
Alpine, NJ 07620

The eighteenth-century historic Kearney House, also known as the Blackledge-Kearney House, contains exhibits and holds public events that reflect Hudson River life. This circa 1750 house was restored to reflect three significant periods in its history: as an eighteenth-century home, a nineteenth-century fishing homestead and the early twentieth-century park headquarters. It is located on the banks of the Hudson River at the Alpine Boat basin in Palisades Interstate Park. Open weekends and holidays, May–October, or by appointment.

Little Red School House Museum

400 Riverside Avenue
Lyndhurst, NJ 07071

This 1893 schoolhouse museum is the headquarters of the Lyndhurst Historical Society, which was established in 1984 to preserve the building. In 1804, Jacob Van Winkle deeded a strip of land to local school trustees for the construction of a school here. The first schoolhouse was erected that same year with money raised by subscription, and thus was born the first known public school system in Bergen County. The Little Red School House is the third schoolhouse built on this site and contains the cupola and bell from the second school, which was built in 1849. The museum, which contains the society's historical collections and changing exhibits, is open year-round and by appointment.

Mahwah Museum, Donald Cooper Railroad and Old Station Museum
201 Franklin Turnpike
Mahwah, NJ 07430

Operated by the Mahwah Museum Society and located in the former Winter Library, this museum offers Mahwah and regional history exhibits and houses documents and artifacts related to Mahwah's past. The collections of artifacts, photographs, historical records and documents are carefully preserved, documented and catalogued and are available by appointment to historians and researchers. The Old Station Museum is located in the original Erie Railroad station building. Museums are opened regularly and by appointment. The Mahwah Museum Society also presents public lecture series and events.

Maywood Station Museum
269 Maywood Avenue
Maywood, NJ 07607

This restored 1872 New York, Susquehanna & Western railroad station, one of the oldest in New Jersey, is located in the heart of Maywood and was added to the NRHP. Restored by the Maywood Station Historical Committee and opened on September 25, 2004, it contains an extensive railroad museum and collections. The site also contains a restored caboose and engine. This accessible museum is open to the public one Sunday a month and for other special events.

Meadowlands Museum
91 Crane Avenue
Rutherford, NJ 07070

The Meadowlands Museum was created to increase people's connection to the heritage of the Meadowlands communities by collecting, preserving, exhibiting and sharing that heritage with the public. Housed in an early nineteenth-century Dutch sandstone farmhouse, one of the few remaining from this period in the Meadowlands area, the museum features changing exhibits of local history and decorative arts, permanent collections of antique toys, pre-electric kitchenware, colonial home crafts, rocks and minerals. The museum is open regularly to the public and holds events throughout the year.

New Jersey Naval Museum—USS *Ling*
78 River Street
Hackensack, NJ 07601

The centerpiece of the New Jersey Naval Museum is the World War II submarine USS *Ling* (SS-297), listed in the State and National Registers of Historic Places and formerly berthed on the Hackensack River in Hackensack. Also on-site are the PBR Mark II, a Vietnam-era river patrol boat; a German Seehund World War II midget two-man submarine; and a World War II Japanese Kaiten Type II. The museum has exhibits on naval history and technology. It was open regularly on weekends for tours and for special events and group visits.

Note: The museum is no longer open to the public, and the artifacts have been distributed to other exhibits. The *Ling* is mired in river muck and destined to eventually be moved to New Orleans.

Old Stone House
538 Island Road
Ramsey, NJ 07446

The Old Stone House was built in the 1700s and is Ramsey's oldest building. It is now the headquarters of the Ramsey Historical Society, which furnishes, maintains and operates the Old Stone House as a museum and educational facility. It is a Dutch sandstone farmhouse with the main floor maintained as an example of Dutch colonial architecture, and the second floor is a Junior Museum. In the early 1950s, the house and property were purchased by the New Jersey Department of Transportation, with the idea to demolish the house to facilitate construction of a Route 17 overpass. The state was persuaded to spare the building thanks to many letters and petitions by the Ramsey Women's Club and others. It is open during the year for tours and events.

Pascack Historical Society Museum
19 Ridge Avenue
Park Ridge, NJ 07656

This Pascack Valley museum, headquarters of the Pascack Historical Society, is located in an 1873 church building that was dedicated by the Reverend Henry Ward Beecher, brother of abolitionist author Harriet Beecher Stowe. Extensive exhibits include a general store, colonial kitchen, dolls, clothing and other displays of American life in the Pascack Valley. A special exhibit features the world's only wampum drilling machine. The society also runs Pascack Adventures, the award-winning program for children. Events, lectures and programs for adults and children are held regularly. Open Sunday and Wednesday afternoons throughout the year.

Pascack Reformed Church Cemetery
65 Pascack Road
Park Ridge, NJ 07656

The Pascack Reformed Church is one of Bergen County's oldest congregations and church buildings. Built in 1813, the front and west sides of the church were constructed of sandstone quarried locally, while fieldstone was used for the rear and east walls. Shortly after the founding of the church, a cemetery was established on the north side of the building. Later, a larger cemetery was established on the south side. These cemeteries contain burials of some of the earliest families in the Pascack Valley, stones with carvings in Dutch, those of early African American families from the area and Native American burials. Open for tours by appointment.

Schoolhouse Museum of the Ridgewood Historical Society
650 East Glen Avenue
Ridgewood, NJ 07451

The one-room schoolhouse in which the museum is housed was built in 1872 and was an operational school until 1905. It now serves as a museum of historic artifacts and is maintained by the Ridgewood Historical Society. Formerly District School No. 45, the museum features various displays that emphasize the historic Saddle River Valley area in the eighteenth and nineteenth centuries, an area that was primarily Dutch when first settled, and rotating exhibits. Open Saturday, Sunday and Thursday by appointment, for school groups and special events.

Van Allen House
Oakland Historical Society
Franklin Avenue and Route 202
Oakland, NJ 07436

This historic house was built by the Van Allen family in 1748 and is in the NRHP. It was known that during the Revolutionary War General George Washington, accompanied by his troops, was here on July 14, 1777, on his way to West Point. Now a museum and headquarters of the Oakland Historical Society, it is open for tours and events during the year, including Dutch Christmas.

Van Voorhees-Quackenbush-Zabriskie House
421 Franklin Avenue
Wyckoff, NJ 07481

This house, possibly the oldest in Wyckoff, is an eighteenth-century Dutch sandstone house with early nineteenth-century additions. The original structure dates back to about 1740, when it was built out of sandstone and fieldstone by William Van Voorhees. His son Albert operated a store and tavern for travelers and the few families in the area. It remained in the Van Voorhees family until 1864 and was sold to Uriah Quackenbush in 1867. The last resident, Uriah's granddaughter Grace Quackenbush Zabriskie, donated the pond in front of the house and five surrounding acres to the town in 1963. The property is now owned by the Borough of Wyckoff and opened regularly during the school year and for special events.

Washington Spring Garden
(Van Saun County Park)
County Historic Site
216 Forest Avenue
Paramus, NJ 07652

This scenic garden setting in the center of Van Saun County Park surrounds a natural spring that was visited by General George Washington during the Steenrapie Encampment of over fourteen thousand American troops in these environs from September 4 to 20, 1780, during the American Revolutionary War. Open during park hours.

Westwood Heritage Society Museum
(Westwood Train Station)
Broadway and Westwood Avenue
Westwood, NJ 07675

The Westwood Museum, which is located in the Westwood Train Station building, was established in 2002 and held its grand opening on Memorial Day 2002. The museum serves as an exhibit gallery for the numerous artifacts of Westwood's past and records of its history that have been acquired or compiled by the society.

Wortendyke Barn

County Historic Site
13 Pascack Road
Park Ridge, NJ 07656

The Wortendyke Barn Museum, a NRHP landmark, is all that remains of the original Wortendyke family farm. The barn, built in 1760, is an outstanding example of the Vernacular architecture referred to as a "New World Dutch Barn," which could be found throughout eighteenth- and nineteenth-century Bergen County. Most were built between 1624 and 1820 wherever Dutch farmers settled along the Hudson, Hackensack, Passaic, Raritan and Mohawk Rivers. The museum's exhibits include handmade eighteenth- and nineteenth-century farm implements and tools, the history of the Wortendyke family farm and exhibits showcasing the agricultural history of Bergen County from the first settlers through the twentieth century. This accessible museum is open Sunday afternoons May–October. Group reservations are available by appointment.

State and National Register of Historic Places and Sites in Bergen County

The National Register of Historic Places is the official list of the nation's historic places worthy of preservation. The New Jersey Register of Historic Places is the official list of the state's historic resources of local, state and national interest and is closely modeled after the National Register Program. The list of Bergen County's State and National Register sites, which can serve as a guide to your visit to Historic Bergen County, may be found on the New Jersey Historic Preservation Office website.

Some other resources:

Bergen Bids
http://www.bergenbids.com

Bergen County Department of Parks
https://www.co.bergen.nj.us/departments-and-services/parks

Bergen County Government Transparency
https://www.co.bergen.nj.us/government-transparency

Bergen County Senior Services
https://www.co.bergen.nj.us/division-of-senior-services

6
CLOSTER

ABRAM DEMAREE HOMESTEAD

Fresh Food Since 1720

Since its first settlers arrived from Europe, Bergen County has been a focal point of trade because of its proximity to New Amsterdam and then New York, the navigable rivers from the Hudson to the Hackensack and Passaic waterways making commerce easy and profitable.

But few areas can boast of a farm that has been supplying food for residents, visitors and travelers for three solid centuries. Closter's Abram Demaree Homestead and Farm could claim the title if there was one available.

Both the homestead and farm, located at the intersection of Old Hook Road and Schraalenburgh Road, are still active food producers and an attraction for passersby, those looking for a tasty field-to-kitchen meal and some terrific "vittles" to take back home.

Although the farm (originally known as the Old Schraalenburgh Farm) is today but a fraction of the size it was in 1720, it grows an abundance of produce for the stream of visitors who enjoy true farm-to-table freshness of corn and a wide variety of vegetables. There are some reports that the farm was established in 1760, but who is going to quibble over a couple of decades when you are dealing with centuries? Some historians date the farm to 1760, but others contend it has existed since 1720.

On the western side of the farm is a shop where you can make those purchases. But don't stop there. You can also buy delicious fresh soup, honey,

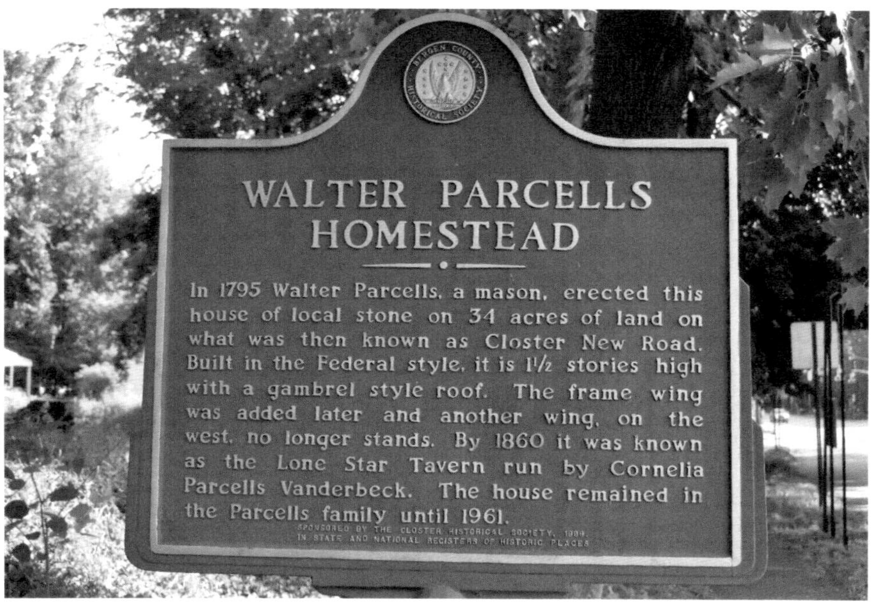

Plaque for what was then the Parcells' Homestead. It later became a tavern and then a farm owned by the Demaree family. There is a disparity in the dates, with the plaque noting it was built in 1795 by Parcells, but a sign at the farmhouse indicates the Demarees were in residence from 1720 on.

With the exception of a string of LED lights on the front, the farmhouse looks much as it did in the early eighteenth century.

Demaree farm across Old Hook Road from the farmhouse. Visitors can purchase produce grown on-site as well as homemade soups and meals.

sandwiches, cakes and more. The prices might be a bit more than your local supermarket with its mass-produced products and veggies that have been shipped in by truck from "who knows where."

In the springtime, the farmers plant corn, tomatoes, lettuce, apples, peppers, blueberries, pumpkins and flowers. There are also eggs from free-range chickens, honey from the farm's own bees, sweet pies and an eight-ounce beef burger. The renovated and air-conditioned café offers both table and takeout service. For those who prefer fresh air there are outdoor tables. Inside during fall and winter, wood-burning stoves provide both heat and ambiance.

The farm stand and café are open Wednesdays through Saturdays from 10:00 a.m. to 6:00 p.m. and on Sundays from 10:00 a.m. until 5:00 p.m.

At the beginning of planting season, passersby can watch the show of rows being furrowed and seeds being planted. There's ample space to park and enjoy the goings-on. But be aware, you will end up in the shop taking vegetables home for dinner.

The Demaree Homestead, listed on the National Register of Historic Places, lies directly across the road from the farm. Here you can buy vintage clothes and other items, some dating back to the nascent era of our country.

Right: Sign proclaiming the "Abram Demaree Homestead" with the earlier date.

Below: An outdoor smokehouse as it would have looked in the eighteenth century. It's near the building but far enough away so as not to present a fire hazard.

There are more modern goods as well, but wander through the rooms and enjoy what is there. There's never pressure to make a purchase, and you can enjoy simply perusing the collection. Both the homestead and farm are run by volunteers, and the operation is full nonprofit.

The site harkens back to 1720, when land was cleared for farming and living quarters. A couple of hundred yards up the road is a huge reservoir where once the navigable Hackensack River flowed. It has long since been diverted.

While the property was first settled in 1720, Abram Demaree bought it in 1760 and operated a general store and tavern there. Its location at the intersection of two major roadways and by the Hackensack River brought customers who could travel there with ease.

In 1809, Abram's son, David, added to the original structure a larger Federal-style house. In the 1970s, the home and farmstead, as was happening to so many other buildings of historical importance, was facing the wrecker's ball of a developer. The land was valuable, the location still prime and the area quite upscale.

A group of preservationists fought a good fight and saved the property from becoming history instead of a historical place. The members were instrumental in having it added to the NRHP. They were aware that many locations of similar historical importance had already ceased to exist.

7

EMERSON

AMERICAN LEGION HALL

The American Legion was formed shortly after World War I as an organization designed to work with and lend assistance to returning veterans. Not too long after, the Veterans of Foreign Wars came into being.

Both organizations worked to protect government benefits for returning military. The Legion and VFW ranks swelled with members, and they were a major force in Washington. While they still hold considerable moral power, their numbers have diminished exponentially since the Korean conflict.

The problem: people just don't join organizations as quickly as they used to. Attend any meeting of the Legion, for example, and there are few World War II vets in attendance, many from Korea and perhaps a handful from current conflicts in the Middle East.

There was always an active post building where the veterans could gather, have social drinks at the bar for reduced costs and attend social events and meetings. Today, many of these posts are little more than memories.

The post hall in Oradell is gone. Ridgefield may be on the way out, and the historic American Legion Post 269 Hall in Emerson is facing not only uncertain times but also the loss of its building.

This hall reflects current and recent conflicts but actually dates to the 1770s, when soldiers used muskets instead of rapid-firing assault rifles. It was then known as the Peter DeBaun House.

Today the building reflects its 250 years and is in serious disrepair. Suggestions ranged from saving a portion of the building to totally

Historic Emerson American Legion Building.

demolishing it and building residences for veterans. While the discussions continue, the building remains, deteriorating one piece at a time.

Under the control of the Bergen County Housing Development Corporation, it is leased by the American Legion for one dollar per year on a ninety-nine-year contract that ran until 2013. The county did build fourteen affordable housing units behind the old structure for veterans with disabilities. Currently, the post has fewer than eighteen members and meets in the Emerson Public Library. The post hall has not been used in several years.

The American Legion and the county drew up an agreement in 2014 to restore the DeBaun House, but after looking into the condition of the building, it was deemed too far gone. The county also notified Emerson that upgrading the building "was not feasible."

The home once stood amid a farm worked by Peter DeBaun and his family. Much of Bergen County in the 1700s was populated by vast farmlands. DeBaun grew crops of grains, potatoes and turnips and had an apple orchard. The house is built in the old Dutch style. But old DeBaun would not recognize his land were he to visit today.

The house stands on what today is 324 Main Street, a combination of side road and main thoroughfare. It passes a large school building and field, a home for Armenian aged and row upon row of private homes.

Peter and his brother, Jacob, were second-generation American born. His family was related to the Harings, a prominent Dutch family. Jacob inherited land from his father, as did Peter. Jacob's home stood a short way down the road, where a large Shop-Rite supermarket stands today.

Peter was born in 1719 over the border in Tappan, New York, and married Miritie Banta, a member of another old and prominent Bergen County family, on August 5, 1743. He built his home sometime between 1765 and 1779. The home was of wood-frame construction with one first-floor room that is now the building's south wing. There was an upstairs garret, or attic, used for storage and possibly as a bed space for one of the family.

The building first appears on the tax map in 1779. The assessment, interestingly, noted that DeBaun owned a slave. Although the Dutch families were not major slaveholders compared with those in the southern portion of the colonies, it was not unusual for them to own other human beings.

With just one slave, it is thought that the enslaved might have shared sleeping quarters with the family or in the garret.

The DeBauns left little in the way of personal information. No letters or other personal documents have ever been uncovered. There was, however, an estate inventory compiled in 1798. Peter had died the previous year, and the list was compiled to determine the value of his estate.

The listing shows that although not wealthy, the DeBauns were of moderate means. No precise value was made.

There was relatively little military action in the DeBaun area. Most of the problems came from both British and Continental troops foraging for food. Indications were that the Continentals were far more voracious than the Brits. With Washington's troops camped along nearby Soldier Hill Road in September 1780, in today's borough of Oradell, they were close enough to raid the fields.

DeBaun presented a bill to the new government for what the troops helped themselves to. He listed, among other items, twenty bushels of buckwheat and corn, five sheep, a heifer, a pig and sixteen "fowls." He valued the loss at fourteen pounds, thirteen shillings.

Jacob fared less favorably, claiming a three-year-old mare, nine sheep, three beehives and three "shoals," all valued at twenty-three pounds, nine shillings.

After Peter DeBaun's death, his property was inherited by his sons, Charles, Jacob and Peter. The land was handed down over the years to various members of the extended family.

Slaveholding continued down the lineage, with the 1830 census indicating a female slave between the ages of thirty and fifty-four, quite a stretch. Also noted was a "free man of color" somewhere between ten and twenty-four years old, most likely the woman's son. New Jersey did not formally abolish slavery until 1846.

The home and property passed from family member to family member and then others until it finally was taken by the American Legion.

8

FAIR LAWN

ICONIC NABISCO PLANT

Sweet Smell of the Morning, Oreos or Animal Crackers?

While Oreos may not be in the National Register of Historic Places, the plant that makes them should be.

For a large portion of Fair Lawn, Glen Rock and Hawthorne residents as well as thousands of drivers passing by on Route 208, the pleasant smells wafting from the plant on the northern side of the highway have been akin to a morning cup of coffee for a wake-up call.

Famed cookie maker Nabisco has been a landmark since it opened in 1958. The huge red letters designating the plant have been visible to passenger aircraft coming in for a landing at the not-too-distant Newark Airport and the even closer general aviation airport, Teterboro.

Residents within sniffing distance would often begin their day by opening the front door to see what was cooking at the plant. It might have been the delicious sandwich cookie Oreo, the often copied but never quite the same Fig Newton, Ritz Crackers, Saltines or, to the delight of children everywhere, Animal Crackers in their distinctive faux circus wagon box. In fact, the Fair Lawn plant became the sole producer of Animal Crackers for Nabisco. So successful was the product that by the mid-1960s, the Fair Lawn plant was producing more than thirty-six million boxes of the treat annually.

Originally located in New York City, Nabisco moved the huge plant to Fair Lawn as one of the original tenants in the McBride Industrial Park, built in

The now closed Nabisco plant that formerly wafted scents of freshly baked Oreo cookies across Route 208 and throughout the neighboring towns.

an old corn field. It was followed by a host of other major companies, such as camera and film maker Kodak.

There was considerable local opposition to the park from residents. Their concerns were realized when Nabisco released air pollutants into what was then a relatively rural countryside. The company later addressed the issue by installing filters that removed most of the chemicals created by the machinery and products.

Town fathers held a different view. The ratables created by Nabisco and other companies were welcomed to assist the tax base. That was especially helpful to provide monies for an ever-growing building for the school population.

Fair Lawn's location, a short distance from bustling New York City and an easy drive from the New Jersey Turnpike, made it an easy decision. Taxes were lower here, there was open space and relocation for employees was almost a no-brainer. On the downside was the growing traffic on Route 208 that made it sometimes look like the world's longest, narrowest parking lot, New York's Long Island Expressway.

While some manufacturing plants invite visitors to come in and watch the production, it couldn't be determined if Nabisco offers such tours. Phone calls to the listed number for the plant went unanswered.

But times change, and in the early days of the twenty-first century, Nabisco began to look for less expensive locations to manufacture its product and moved the Fig Newton brand to Mexico. Saltines remained in the United States but were shifted to less expensive manufacturing markets. While the company said it would spend millions of dollars to upgrade the plant and make it more profitable, the number of employees in Fair Lawn plummeted from more than one thousand to six hundred. Not a good sign for continued work. Nabisco's parent company, Mondelez, seems to be on a track to close the plant. The company wants to consolidate its facilities, and the old manufacturing equipment in Fair Lawn may never see the millions suggested for improvement.

While company officials continue to deny that any firm decision has been made, contending that it is only a "consideration," local officials and Governor Phil Murphy have been lobbying to retain the facility.

OLD NAUGLE HOUSE

Going…Going…Gone?

Preservationists in Bergen County have been fighting what amounts to an all-out war against developers who have set their sights on any number of historic properties in the county. Fair Lawn's Naugle House, constructed between the 1740s and 1750s (the exact date is undetermined), is today surrounded by hurricane fencing and the possibility of becoming condos.

Standing forlornly at the entrance to the Saddle River County Park at Dunkerhook Road, it is a crumbling edifice protected from vandals and those without a sense of history. Although the house was added to the NRHP on January 9, 1983, following its designation as a historic location, a lack of maintenance has brought it to a point where developers can argue that it is too expensive to repair and maintain.

Those out for a walk in the county park or bicyclists pedaling by barely give it a glance. It's just another of the many old stone houses in Bergen County. But for those with a sense of history, they see another piece of our heritage going the way of the wrecker's ball. Once reduced to rubble, there is no going back.

The stone house is located on a low hillside along the path into the park from Dunkerhook Road and was the subject of a visit by the National Park Heritage Documentation Program Historic American Buildings Survey to

The Naugle House, a historic building slated for renovation. Naugle served as Lafayette's paymaster for the Frenchman's Light Military Division in the Revolution. Lafayette visited the building in 1824.

take photographs and prepare historical architectural drawings. But that was in 1938, when the structure was in habitable condition. Some forty-five years later, in 1983, the National Park Service added the building to the National Register of Historic Places.

The Naugle House was built by Jacob Vanderbeek Jr., almost adjacent to another home he built, now known as the Jacob Vanderbeek Jr. House. Both buildings are typical of the old Dutch Colonial style that was popular in the 1600s and 1700s. That was not a stretch, as the Dutch were early settlers throughout the region, and most of the homes were built in that common style. Most of the walls were of sandstone blocks. The Naugle House, however, is uncommon in that it was built into a hillside, whereas most of the Dutch Colonial homes were on level ground and part of farmlands. And while many of those homes were single story, the Naugle House held a second floor.

As was also common in those days, the lower floor was used as a kitchen encased in the stone walls. The upper level is of wood-frame construction. It is quite similar to another contemporary building, the Zabriskie-Tenant House, across the Saddle River in what is now the Borough of Paramus.

Its location near the entrance to Saddle River County Park and the many people passing by have made the Naugle House a recognizable landmark and piece of history.

While George Washington may have slept his way around Bergen County, there's no indication he ever visited the Naugle House. That being said, there is some evidence that the house was visited in 1784 by the young Frenchman and friend of Washington the Marquis de Lafayette.

Hoping to preserve the historical building, in 2010, the Borough of Fair Lawn purchased it for the princely sum of $1.7 million with a combination of funds from Fair Lawn, Bergen County and the state's Open Space and Green Acres program. The hope was to both preserve the historic building and keep an area of green space in perpetuity. The purchase was spurred in large part after plans were revealed that a builder was intent on constructing town houses on the site.

The following year, both Fair Lawn and Bergen County held a dedication ceremony for the Naugle House. Also in 2011, Preservation New Jersey placed the Naugle House on its list of "The Ten Most Endangered" historic sites. It has been targeted for demolition and neglect as a connection to development plans for the Jacob Vanderbeek Jr. House. Should that come to fruition, the Naugle House would be surrounded by a modern parking lot. That construction would surround the house and potentially endanger its structural integrity as well as the landscape.

There is a group of historic preservationists pushing to keep the Naugle House for coming generations to visit, enjoy and remember Bergen County's history.

RADBURN PLANNED URBAN DEVELOPMENT

A Community within Another Community and a Respite from the Hustle

Those looking for the lost city of Shangri-La might have found it in the quiet community of Radburn, situated in the heart of the borough of Fair Lawn. With all the aura of a gated development, Radburn is the antithesis of that concept.

Radburn was named to the NRHP in 1975 and then designated a National Historic Landmark in 2005.

Its open space, rolling green public lawns and public walkways are as inviting to both residents and guests as a miniature Central Park.

But that was not always the case.

From its opening in 1927 and for more than twenty years, Radburn was not only unwelcoming to some segments of the general population but also systematically excluded almost all non-White and virtually any Jewish people. This discrimination was unofficially accepted by Radburn's founders and enforced by the community's administration and real estate agents.

"Undesirable" potential residents didn't face any written policy or regulation but were victims of "steering" by local real estate agents and those employed by Radburn's developer, the City Housing Corp.

The exclusionary policy was not seen as such by the perpetrators, nor did they consider it prejudicial or overtly racist. Their theory was simply that this was a community, that although supposedly economically and socially diverse, if residents were more alike than different, more cohesive than of differing racial and religious backgrounds, the residents would be more content with their lives and community.

Although the Supreme Court later held that such covenants were unconstitutional and illegal, there were ways and means of excluding Jewish and Black families.

Social workers contended that any decision on the exclusionary policies should be determined by the residents and not the developers. Residents chose to be welcoming.

Such a policy may have worked in those days when entertainers such as Al Jolson could go on stage and perform in Blackface. Jolson could not do that today, and racial/ethnic/religious exclusionary covenants would elicit immediate court hearings and severe sanctions.

The early elitists would be horrified to see the inclusive community that is today's Radburn. When Jewish people were finally able to make it through the main gate (the gate was a virtual barrier rather than a physical entity), they came, not in droves, but today there are substantial numbers of all peoples. Well-known architect Steven Ehrlich; Professor Phillip Plotch; and one of the country's most prolific baseball writers, Dan Schlossberg, and his wife, Phyllis, were welcomed.

To what would have been the chagrin of those early exclusionists, Radburn is surrounded by an enclave of Russians who just happen to be Jewish. A huge synagogue on Century Road caters to this growing population, something that would have been anathema in Radburn's early years.

A quiet, narrow Radburn street with homes built closely together.

Historic Radburn Plaza Building, a symbol of the planned urban development (PUD).

Radburn was an oxymoron. It was designed to be diverse both socially and economically but in fact was more like a private club.

Plans for the creation of Radburn would have created what planners and developers referred to as a "PUD," a planned urban development. The concept was of small enclaves that would have a variety of housing, schools, commerce and perhaps jobs, all within walking distance. It would have been, in their concept, an American Garden City modeled after similar projects in Europe.

The PUD would have reduced urban congestion, provided safe lanes for pedestrians to avoid danger from passing vehicles and allowed residents to connect with nature and develop mutual relationships with neighbors. The majority of homes either fronted huge green spaces or had openings from the rear that encircled that space.

While most developers build projects on a grid plan, Radburn was unique in that homes were constructed around the green spaces. Many of the homes fronted narrow streets that discouraged speeding cars and provided little on-street parking. Residents were expected to park in their individual driveways. The majority of streets were dead-ended, with no lane for through traffic.

The community was originally meant to be an experimental development with a focus on pedestrian access to shared indoor and outdoor open

Children at play on Radburn's common ground.

spaces. Radburn is immediately seen as separate and distinct in design from its surrounding area. It was arguably the first such development and set the standard for those to come, including Greenbelt, Maryland; Reston, Virginia; and Village Green in Los Angeles.

Radburn today is an unincorporated community surrounded by the borough of Fair Lawn. It was specifically designed to separate traffic and pedestrians with a system of roads whereby pedestrians do not cross any major motorways at grade level. It introduced the so-called residential superblock and is believed to have been one of the original incorporators of the cul-de-sac.

Today there are just over three thousand residents in Radburn living in shy of 500 single-family homes, 48 town houses, 30 two-family buildings, one 93-unit apartment complex and a subsequent 165-unit section of town homes.

Radburn encompasses 149 acres, including 23 acres of open space parkland. There are four tennis courts, three baseball fields, two softball fields and two swimming pools. For the much younger set there are two "toddler" playgrounds and a bathing pool. Radburn has its own community center, library, gymnasium, club room, preschool and maintenance facilities. There is also an elementary school that is open to the entire borough.

There is a degree of autonomy for Radburn. The Radburn Association, the PUD's governing body, is empowered to set and collect fees from residents for the maintenance of the common properties, monitor development and restrict decorations so as to keep an ordered look to the community.

While nonresidents are free to visit the green spaces and are permitted free range throughout the community, only residents may use the facilities.

The association was a self-perpetuating body until 2017, when board membership was opened to all residents.

9

FORT LEE

PALISADES HISTORIC PARK

History with a View

Resting atop the Palisades, overlooking the Hudson River and New York City, is Fort Lee Historic Park. The park is dedicated to preserving the memory of a fort built to protect sections of the newly rebellious nation and as an educational tool for future generations.

General George Washington ordered two forts to be built on opposite shores of the Hudson River to prevent the British navy from sailing up the river and dividing our newly formed nation. They were built overlooking a narrow part of the river that was used to ferry individuals and commerce between the two states. In June 1776, the area where the future Fort Washington would be built was inspected by General Washington, and the decision was made to go ahead with construction. It was felt that the two forts, Fort Washington on the New York side and Fort Constitution on the New Jersey side, would be able to bombard British vessels moving upriver and seeking to control the area. In addition, ships and other impediments were sunk between the two forts to help block the river and make passage more difficult.

Had the British been able to move upriver unimpeded, they would have been able to take Albany and put a serious crimp in the rebels' ability to fight.

Right: Monument to Revolutionary War drummers and flag bearers. The high-rise in the background offers a startling comparison.

Below: Heavy cannon aimed over the Hudson River to defend against British ships heading north. In the background is the George Washington Bridge, today's prime route between New Jersey and New York.

Ironically, the coat of arms on the cannon represents British royalty, King George, and in all likelihood was a spoil of war captured by the American rebels and moved to the defense of the Hudson River.

Originally, Fort Constitution was to be built near the water under the direction of General Mercer. It was later decided to move it up to the top of the Palisades, and in July 1776, under the direction of Commander Joseph Philips of the New Jersey State Militia, the newly positioned fort was constructed. Fort Constitution was later named Fort Lee, in honor of General Charles Lee, a successful leader of the Continental army.

During the short lifespan of the forts, several British warships were fired on and damaged by artillery from both sides. The British commander General Howe ordered the capture of both. Fort Washington was captured by Lieutenant General Lord Cornwallis on November 16 using Hessian as well as British forces. He was aided in his attack by William Demont, a deserter who had been a principal aide (adjutant) to Colonel Robert Magaw. Demont defected with the plans, information about the ships and other barriers sunk in the Hudson River as well as the defenses of Fort Washington. Of the 2,800 soldiers captured, 2,000 later died while captive.

With the capture of Fort Washington in New York and the apprehension of almost 2,800 Continental troops, Fort Lee became redundant. Even with the two forts, control of the Hudson did not prove successful—with only one, even less so. Commander in Chief of the Royal Forces William Howe ordered General Lord Cornwallis to capture Fort Lee. Two days later, on November 20, a force of more than 4,000 troops—British, Hessians and Loyalists—were ferried across the river and landed several miles north of the fort. They marched overland to attack the fort. Washington learned of the landing of the British forces and ordered the abandonment of Fort Lee. It could no longer serve the purpose for which it was intended, and the men would be needed in later battles. The fort was speedily evacuated, with Washington's primary purpose to preserve the lives of the Continental forces. Artillery pieces, ammunition, stores and provisions were left in place due to the immediate evacuation of the fort. Equipment and provisions were lost, but the lives of the defenders were preserved. Out of roughly 2,000 troops, only 250 were captured. The rest were able to flee west through New Bridge to parts of New Jersey and across the Delaware River, living to fight another day.

Cornwallis did not swiftly pursue the rebel troops, allowing them to escape. It was a blunder that would cost the British the war. The Continentals' route away has come to be known as the "Washington Retreat" and passed through several Bergen County communities, along what is now Newbridge Road bordering New Milford and Teaneck. They crossed over a bridge and into what is the current Newbridge Landing Historic Park, which contains several period buildings. While the old bridge is gone, a new one has replaced it, and some of the wooden pilings can still be seen jutting from the river.

It was during this time that Thomas Paine wrote his pamphlet *The Crisis*, containing the immortal words, "These are the times that try men's souls."

On driving onto the grounds of the park, located in Fort Lee, one parks in a metered lot. Immediately on disembarking, one sees the Fort Lee Historic Park Visitors Center. A short visit to the center with its many historical displays gives a visitor an excellent introduction to the area and what can be seen. There are artifacts of both the colonial army and from British forces.

This cooking mini-hut doesn't look like much, and it's not a barbecue, but it was critical in providing hot meals for the rebels stationed at Fort Lee Historic Park.

There is also a small shop offering souvenirs depicting the period. Exiting the visitor center, one should head south to walk among the reconstructed sections of the fort. The paths are well paved, and the walking is easy and accessible to all.

Various buildings, reproduced to size, that would have been found within the fort have been rebuilt. Soldiers' quarters, a blockhouse, a storage building and cooking facilities are some of the structures on display.

Walking along the ramparts and looking over to the river, it is easy to understand why the fort was constructed here. One can walk along several artillery battery positions that were reconstructed, showing the strategic views those manning the guns had across the river and to New York. These are the Barbette Batteries, where the cannon and mortars were fired over the defensive walls rather than through spaces within them. There is extensive signage, with illustrations, explaining what one is seeing along the paths.

Walking away from the side of the fort facing the river, you can view a small section of the musketry breastworks atop a steep hill. These breastworks face westward in the direction that foot soldiers and cavalry would have had to take when attacking the fort. It would be along this path that the British army and its allies would have had to travel, since the high and vertical cliffs of the Palisades at that location are difficult and impractical to scale.

From the ramparts, one can enjoy the views overlooking New York City and the George Washington Bridge. The paths throughout the park provide easy walking for all. There is a road leading down to where one can view the George Washington Bridge looking up.

10

HACKENSACK

SEARS BUILDING

A Hit with Cowboys, A Memory for Bergen County

Just short of a century old, the iconic Sears (Roebuck) department store that was the anchor of the Hackensack business district is a fond memory to some and a financial disaster to other merchants. After eighty-seven years and several threatened closings, the huge gray building at the northern reaches of the county seat has finally closed its doors.

Sears outlasted the Old West, the Pony Express and the Indian Wars, but it finally succumbed to steady advance of progress and online shopping.

And that's quite ironic, because Sears was one of two great "shop-by-mail" commercial entities. The other was long-gone Montgomery Ward; both were founded by Chicago natives.

They pioneered mail-order purchasing and then began opening their iconic stores. Montgomery Ward was the first to vanish, while Sears, dropping the "Roebuck," soldiered on. It had a reputation for quality clothing, electronic equipment and appliances. There was a no-questions-asked policy for returns and refunds, a policy that cost Sears dearly in the long-term.

There were attempts by Sears's parent company, Sears Holdings/Transform Holdco LLC, to close the beloved store. Local pressure from both merchants and shoppers managed to keep the old boy afloat for a number of years. The fear of local merchants was that with the anchor store gone, business would fall off even more than it had in recent years, with shoppers in increasing numbers heading for the proliferation of giant malls in Bergen County and for the computers in their homes for online shopping.

They were right. With the closure of the building at the entrance to Hackensack's commercial district, stores began to close. The pandemic could be blamed for much of it. Sears stores in other locations in New Jersey have been shuttered. In 2018, the company filed for bankruptcy. One Sears in nearby Jersey City may remain open and would be the only one remaining in the state. While there were others, the Hackensack location was the oldest and the most visible.

The huge gray building, sitting at the head of the city's main street and its major north–south roadway, Hackensack Avenue, was visible from a distance and immediately announced that you were coming into the business district.

The building at the north end of the large parking lot was occupied by Sears Auto Center. Today it is an Aldi Supermarket.

Sitting like the Gibraltar of Main Street, Sears has been the greeting for shoppers coming into Hackensack since 1932. In an effort to remain viable, it downsized when it sold the parcel to German-operated Aldi.

Today the Sears building stands much like a massive gray mausoleum—another part of Bergen County consigned to history.

SUBMARINE USS *LING*

Going…Going…Gone

Not all military veterans have won their stripes in combat. Many served in peacetime, others served behind the lines and still others came online as combat was winding down.

Such was the case with the submarine USS *Ling*, although the boat (submarines are classified as boats rather than ships) was awarded a Battle Star, indicating it saw action.

The *Ling* sat, mired in the muck and mud of the Hackensack River about a block north of the county courthouse and just above the Court Street Bridge. Following the devastation of Superstorm Sandy, the *Ling* and adjacent Submarine Museum were closed, ending years of delight for Scouting groups and other visitors who made pilgrimages to climb down the ladder to its interior, see how submariners lived and fought and, perhaps, pretend that they too were off on a mission.

This page: One of the few remaining Balao-class submarines, the USS *Ling* sits forlornly at its mooring on the Hackensack River. Its hull is rusted through, and vandals severely damaged its interior. It was forced from its mooring by the Borg family to be replaced by a residential development.

The *Ling*, named for a fish, was built at Cramp Shipbuilding Company of Philadelphia. Its keel was laid on November 2, 1942, and the vessel was launched on August 15, 1943. It was finally commissioned on June 8, 1945, too late for World War II. It was decommissioned a scant few months later on October 28, 1945. The boat was lastly struck from the navy on December 1, 1971. On October 19, 1978, it was added to the National Register of Historic Places.

The Balao-class submarine launched 120 boats, the most of any submarine classification. The first was named the USS *Balao*, thus the name for its class, as is naval custom. Of that number only a handful still exist, and they are in repose at various historical sites as attractions. They are *Batfish*, *Becuna*, *Clamagore*, *Lionfish*, *Pampanito* and *Razorback*.

While *Ling* never saw combat, others of its class were in the thick of battle. The *Tang* was captained by one of the most famous sub commanders, Richard O'Kane, who had thirty-one kills to his record. O'Kane was a Medal of Honor recipient. Tragically, the *Tang* was sunk by one of its own torpedoes that went awry, but not until it had sunk 227,800 tons of enemy shipping.

After its decommissioning, the *Ling* reposed in the reserve until a concerted effort by the Submarine Memorial Association managed to acquire it. The 312-foot, 2,500-ton boat was brought up the Hackensack River to its mooring between a diner and the bridge in January 1973. The property was leased for one dollar a year. The Borg family, former owner of the *Bergen Record*, later determined that the land was valuable for development and sought to retake it from the museum. There was no lease, and the facility was there basically on a month-to-month basis.

On the land side of the river stood a trailer that was home to the Submarine Memorial Association. There were numerous artifacts on the property ranging from a torpedo to a submarine deck gun. Inside the trailer were more fragile objects relating to both submarines and naval ships. The site and the boat became popular destinations for school groups and other organizations.

Following the devastating storm, the museum was closed, and access to the boat was shut down. Since the *Ling* sat in the river rather than on dry land, neither the Borg family nor the City of Hackensack expressed any interest in expending funds for its preservation or relocation. The museum shut down, and the property took on the look of an abandoned city lot, with refuse and litter rather than submarine artifacts on display.

Over time and from lack of attention and maintenance, the *Ling*'s exterior began to suffer from the elements. In December 2016, a plea was made to the Borgs, the City of Hackensack and the State of New Jersey. The response from all was that which many human veterans received from officialdom: "Not interested." The *Record*, a daily newspaper owned by the Borgs, was sold to the Gannett newspaper chain and had zero interest in preservation of the boat.

Complicating matters, the boat had not been dry docked since being moored on the Hackensack in the 1970s, and no maintenance of any consequence was performed. Over the years, the *Ling* sank into the muck of the river. Then along came the superstorm and complicated matters.

The museum shut down, visitors stopped coming and the boat fell into greater disrepair. The museum was expected to vacate the property in August 2018. Before the museum could do anything, a group of vandals broke into the *Ling* on August 14, 2018. They stole several plaques from the boat, damaged artifacts that were still inside the sub, broke gears and controls and then, for some very sick reason, opened petcocks and filled the sub with the murky waters of the Hackensack River, causing tens of thousands of dollars in damage.

It took a while, but the vandals were finally identified and arrested. Then again, five other vandals broke into the sub and stole several more artifacts.

That only intensified the problems facing the *Ling*. With the museum gone, transported to an uncertain fate in Kentucky, and the landside property getting set for development, there was no question but that the boat would have to either be moved or dismantled. But first, thousands of dollars in damages would have to be addressed.

Military veterans came to the rescue of the *Ling*. They began to pump the water out so that the damage could be assessed and perhaps repaired. There was up to fourteen feet of river water inside the hull. Original equipment such as radios, electronics, mess kits, uniforms and bunks and mattresses were soaked. A concrete company on the east side of the river loaned the volunteers a submersible pump and an air compressor to help in draining the water from the sub's interior. The air compressor was used to blow out the ballast tanks with the hope the sub could once again float.

Much of the work was accomplished by members of the Louisville (KY) Naval Museum. They had an ulterior motive. The hope was that the sub could be raised from the muck and floated down the Hackensack River to a point whereby it could be floated to New Orleans, where it would be lifted onto a commercial barge. It would be floated to a Jeffersonville, Indiana shipyard—at no charge.

The *Ling* would be placed in dry dock and refurbishment would begin. The price for dry docking ranges from an estimated $1 million to $2 million.

That's on top of the estimated $1 million for the barge trip from Hackensack to New Orleans. But to the volunteers, it would be worth every cent of the cost to save an artifact from World War II.

The goal is to bring the boat back to its original condition and make one last move—across the river to a new and permanent naval museum in Louisville.

To accomplish all of this, a major task remains. Literally millions of dollars must be raised for repair and to construct an appropriate display. The *Ling* is now a wonderful memory of what Bergen County had and lost.

THE COUNTY GREEN

The county courthouse and green are central to many communities. Today, the classically designed Bergen County Courthouse functions strictly as a justice center. It originally housed both courtrooms and Bergen's administrative offices. A new multimillion-dollar administrative building now serves the business functions.

Across from what originally was the main entrance to the courthouse is a small green with a statue dedicated to Revolutionary War hero General Enoch Poor and a statue of a soldier with the look of a man ready to defend

Opposite: The modern courthouse, a classically designed building.

Above: Original Bergen County Courthouse. The red-brick building to the right is the only section still standing. It is known today as the Mansion House and is home to law offices.

Right: Old church across from the courthouse. Its cemetery holds the bodies of prominent people in the county's history.

his country. The church across the road has a cemetery adjacent with remains of many dating back to the Revolution, including General Poor.

The church has an adjacent cemetery holding the bodies of many people prominent in the early days of the county. General Poor lies in repose here.

Not far away is the old People's Trust Bank building, once the tallest structure in the county. After several iterations of being absorbed by mergers with other banking institutions, it was converted into upscale condos in the heart of the city.

HOLLY'S ICE CREAM PARLOR/COACH HOUSE DINER

Ice Cream to Green Salad

Souvenir matchbook covers from Holly's Ice Cream Parlor.

Driving east on State Route 4, a major link to New York City via the George Washington Bridge, was one of the most popular hangouts for teens on dates and families out for an evening of enjoyment.

Holly's Ice Cream Parlor and Restaurant served up the best dessert in Northern New Jersey. Its pale-green exterior was matched by the painted interior décor. Visitors could sit on swivel stools at the counter as they waited for their ice cream sodas or sundaes. Groups and families took up residence in booths.

For those looking for something to eat before dessert, there were a variety of hamburgers and a short list of other comfort foods. But good things often don't last. Holly's was sold and a diner constructed in its place. Oddly, perhaps the ghosts of past Holly's guests getting revenge, shortly after the new diner opened, it burned down.

But the future was brighter. Greek restaurateur George Pappas stepped in and rebuilt the diner, opening the new Coach House on the old Holly's site. Like most Greek-operated diners there was an extensive menu. But Pappas was hands-on and moved in and out of the kitchen overseeing everything. His top waiter, Rahman, kept track of guests from regulars to sporadic diners and greeted each as old friends. It truly was like Holly's reincarnated.

Holly's was replaced by the Coach House Diner and Restaurant in its prime location on Route 4 and Hackensack Avenue. It has become a mecca for celebrities passing on the way to New York. Astronaut Tom Jones stopped by and posed with the eatery's hostess, Linda.

The Coach House, noted for its food and service, and its owner, George Pappas, has become a destination for both locals and passersby on the highway. Some have even said they can smell the ice cream from Holly's. More likely it's the Coach House's sundaes.

The Coach House is often host to politicians, entertainers and celebrities stopping on their way to New York or local officials who conduct municipal business in its booths. One of the celebrities who stopped there was astronaut Tom Jones, who flew on four space shuttle missions and during a spacewalk helped build the space station.

Unlike other diner/restaurants, Pappas does not line his walls with pictures of famous people who have dined there. He prefers to give them a degree of anonymity. Jones was captured on film by someone who recognized him and managed to catch a photo.

HACKENSACK UNIVERSITY MEDICAL CENTER

Bank to Condos

At the other end of the city was Hackensack University Medical Center. Starting as a wooden building, it has grown to become the largest part of the Meridian Health System and one of the top medical facilities in New Jersey. It now encompasses acres of ground and offers treatment for everything from a broken toe to major cancer surgery. Today it is known as Hackensack Meridian University Medical Center. Compared with other hospitals in the county, it has the appearance more of a big-city hospital.

Modern Hackensack Hospital campus, now known as Hackensack Meridian University Medical Center.

The original Hackensack Hospital in a wooden building.

Early Hackensack Hospital.

Above: People's Trust Building with street lined with vintage cars, mid-1920s.

Opposite: For many years the tallest building in the county, originally People's Trust Bank, it was merged with other banking institutions until it was sold to a private developer. Today it houses luxury condos.

On Main Street stands a building that was once the tallest in Bergen County. Originally the main office of the People's Trust Bank, it went through a number of changes as it merged with other banks until the financial institutions finally moved out. Today it towers over the city's Main Street as upscale condo units.

11

HO-HO-KUS

THE HERMITAGE

With all the history of our country in Bergen County, it's difficult to find one location that might just offer more than others. It will obviously be a controversial statement in view of what so many towns in the county have to offer.

The fact that George Washington slept in any particular place or made one home his temporary headquarters abounds throughout Bergen County. It does have the reputation as "The Crossroads of the Revolution," after all.

But all that being said, the Hermitage is special.

The fourteen-room Gothic Revival structure, originally built in 1747, is not by any means one of the oldest buildings in the county. A number would be great-great-grandfathers to the Hermitage.

Interestingly, the estate, more than two-and-a-half centuries old, lays claim to the British in the Revolutionary War and, at the same time, quartered General George Washington.

After the French and Indian War, the property was purchased by James Marcus Prevost, a British army officer. As the Revolution took root, Prevost was called back to active duty, leaving his wife, Theodosia, and their five children to maintain the property, a rather tenuous job, as she was surrounded by the rebels. But she was an inventive person.

Bergen County had numerous families and individuals who were loyal to the Crown, the so-called Tories. Theodosia Prevost's loyalties made her

The Hermitage in Ho-Ho-Kus holds a lot of history, including the wedding of Vice President Aaron Burr.

rather unpopular with the Revolutionaries. But she had a knack for dealing with both sides and managed to survive and keep the property intact.

The area, especially nearby Paramus, was rife with military activity as the war waged on. Both British and Patriots made a habit of raiding farms and fueling up on crops, meats and other provisions to keep them going. Rarely was any form of payment made. As a side event, both armies made a regular habit of raiding the other side.

Theodosia invited George Washington and some of his officers to the Hermitage shortly after the Battle of Monmouth in 1778. At the same time, Washington was involved in the courts-martial of General Charles Lee at nearby Paramus First Church.

The general made the Hermitage his headquarters for four days. Among his staff were Alexander Hamilton, John Laurens and the Marquis de Lafayette.

While her husband was off fighting Washington's troops, Theodosia formed a close "friendship" with future vice president Aaron Burr, who was later to gain infamy when he shot and killed Hamilton in a duel.

The couple soon developed what could then be described as an "intimate friendship." Following the war, James Marcus Prevost died, and Theodosia and Aaron Burr not only brought their relationship out in the open but also married at the Hermitage in 1782. To say the least, the pair, especially Theodosia—with the mores of the time more focused on such activities by women rather than men—met with considerable criticism and disapproval.

Following the Revolution, a long list of owners had possession of the Hermitage, and for a time it was used as a tavern. In 1807, it was purchased by a young doctor, Elijah Rosencrantz, and his wife, Cornelia Sutton. A long period of occupation by that family ensued, as four generations actually lived at the Hermitage.

In the 1820s, the industrious doctor, inspired by industrialization in the nearby city of Paterson, built a cotton mill alongside the Ho-Ho-Kus Brook. The family owned and operated the mill for more than six decades.

Architect William H. Ranleff was brought in during the 1847–48 period to design and renovate the building. What was the original stone farmhouse was totally redone, a new wing was added and the house was given what were then modern amenities, including running water and heat.

After the turn of the century, in 1917, the current resident, Bess Rosencrantz, seeking income, opened the front parlor of the Hermitage as a tearoom. Working with her sister, Mary Elizabeth, the two poured tea commercially for more than ten years. Mary Elizabeth was in charge of the

Guest building or servant's quarters near the main building at the Hermitage.

kitchen and planned menus. Bess acted as hostess, entertaining visitors with stories of the Hermitage's past.

Mary Elizabeth was the last of the Rosencrantzes to live in the historic building. She died in March 1970 and willed the house and five acres of the grounds, along with all contents of house and property, to the State of New Jersey. That same year, the Hermitage was designated a National Historic Landmark. The following year, 1971, it was added to the New Jersey Register of Historic Places.

Today it is maintained by the Friends of the Hermitage, a nonprofit group, in conjunction with the state. Tours are offered for a fee.

12

LITTLE FERRY

GETHSEMANE CEMETERY

At its founding, Gethsemane Cemetery in Little Ferry was known as the "Colored Cemetery." Looking into the cemetery, a visitor will see well-maintained grounds and plaques explaining its history. Very few grave markers remain, as years have taken a heavy toll.

In 1860, land was deeded by three White men for use by the "colored" population of the village of Hackensack as a cemetery. In 1901, the Gethsemane Cemetery Association Inc. was formed with the ownership transferred to Black trusteeship.

Over five hundred individuals were buried between 1866 and 1924. Extensive church records and those from funeral homes exist, identifying those within its grounds. Within the cemetery are buried two Civil War veterans who fought in a Connecticut "colored" regiment; their markers can no longer be found.

One of the tombstones that can be seen is that of Elizabeth Dulfer. She was born a slave, freed and became a businesswoman. She bought and amassed extensive land holdings containing clay deposits. An astute businesswoman, Dulfer hired workers who turned the clay into building bricks, earning her a fortune. At the time of her death, she was one of the wealthiest women in Bergen County. During the cemetery's active lifetime, White people were also buried within the grounds.

Elizabeth, after being freed, married three times. Her last husband was John Dulfer, a White Dutchman who was thirty-three years her junior.

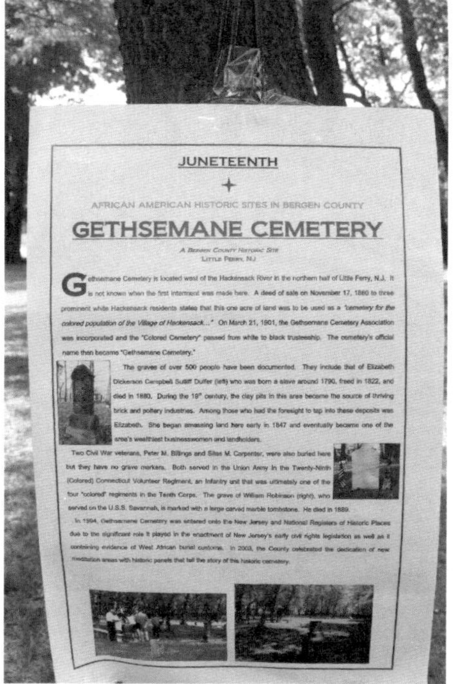

Left: Information sign at Gesthemane Cemetery, burial ground for slaves, former slaves and other non-White people.

Right: Grave marker for Elizabeth Dulfer, a former slave who died at ninety years old in 1880. She won her freedom and became an entrepreneur, dying a wealthy woman. She married several times; her last husband, John Dulfer, was a White Dutchman thirty-three years her junior. She purchased land others thought worthless because it was all clay. She turned the clay into building blocks and began investing in business and property.

Elizabeth became an entrepreneur. She purchased land that was little more than a clay pit, but she saw opportunity. She had clay dug up and baked into bricks that she sold. From there, she began to invest in a variety of businesses, and her fortune grew. She died a wealthy woman in 1880 at the age of ninety.

In 1894, the New Jersey legislature passed the "Negro Burial Bill," desegregating burials in state cemeteries. The bill was introduced and passed as a result of the controversy surrounding the refusal of the burial of Samuel Bass, a sextant of the Hackensack First Baptist Church, in a White cemetery.

As a result of private individuals and organizations that sought to preserve the cemetery, Bergen County eventually took over control and brought it back to the condition it deserved and is currently in. Archaeological

View across the cemetery, showing only a handful of markers remaining. In the early days, it was not always considered necessary to leave markers for non-White interments.

studies have taken place above and below ground and are continuing. The exploration of the grounds has recovered artifacts connecting some of the African American burials with customs traceable to Africa. In addition, ground-penetrating radar has been used to map where bodies were interred.

Every year on Juneteenth, June 19, there is a guided tour of the cemetery to mark emancipation in Bergen County.

13

MAHWAH

MAHWAH MUSEUM

Recycling History

Recycling virtually everything today to save the environment is a common happenstance. It was an activity that was never even thought of centuries ago. Fortunately, our forebears didn't dispose of things that today we consider of historical importance.

Many buildings ranging back centuries have been saved from the wrecker's ball and have been repurposed for modern times. While the Mahwah Museum may not have the patina of the older buildings, its exhibits bring you back in time to pre-Revolutionary days and up to the modern—or near modern—day with permanent exhibits. The building housing the museum was originally used as the Mahwah Public Library and was built in 1949. The exhibits contained in the building range from Revolutionary times to the present and are all artfully displayed.

One of the borough's most famous residents, guitarist and composer Les Paul of the famed Les Paul and Mary Ford duo, lived, played and composed here.

Paul, born Lester William Polsfuss in Waukesha, Wisconsin, was a longtime resident of Mahwah and composed many of his popular songs there. Paul worked with Mary Ford, his second wife, until their divorce, after which his production and popularity waned.

But his connection to Mahwah was so solid that the Mahwah Museum has created a permanent exhibit showcasing his career, guitars and music. On exhibit are many of his guitars, his recording studio and inventions that he either developed himself or helped develop for the music and recording industry, such as the electric guitar, a mainstay of today's music.

The Les Paul exhibit is on permanent display at the museum. Visitors can learn about his work on sound-on-sound recording and development of the electric guitar. There is also a display of one-of-a-kind guitars made especially for Paul. They are set around a re-creation of the studio in which he worked.

Before Les Paul had his reel-to-reel tape deck in 1949, he did his recordings on a lathe he made. He used acetate discs and recorded such popular songs as "Lover," "Nola" "and "Goofus." The museum is the proud possessor of both that lathe and Paul's reel-to-reel tape deck, now on display at the museum.

On display are also a 1995 Les Paul–Jimmy Page guitar, a 1987 Les Paul Standard Guitar and a 1969 Les Paul Custom guitar from his personal collection.

While Paul is often credited with development of the electric guitar, Freddy Fender actually beat him to market with his own creation. Purists note that Fender may have commercialized it, but Paul invented it.

Nearby is the Old Station and Caboose at 142 North Railroad Avenue, both well worth visiting. The Mahwah Museum Society was founded in 1965 and converted the Winter Public Library building into a museum.

During the year, special programs regarding the work of Les Paul and Mary Ford are presented. On the same floor is an interesting exhibit devoted to Ramapo College showing a dorm room from 1965 to 1975, with life-size "students" in a realistic setting.

A portion of the main floor is also devoted to a presentation in miniature of the Palisades Amusement Park. The last two are temporary exhibits.

Going downstairs, along the walls are photographs taken by Lee Vold, who, after moving to Mahwah, became the "official" photographer, recording practically every activity taking place in town.

Downstairs visitors are treated to an amazing working model train exhibit that covers almost half of the floor surface. Several train sets run along various levels, featuring scenes of where the real trains would run.

Follow up the museum visit with a short walk to the Old Station Museum building and the Caboose.

The Old Station Museum was established in a building that originally served as a station for the Erie Railroad. It had been slated for demolition but was rescued by the Winters family and then taken by the Mahwah Historical Society.

Railroad memorabilia collectors donated numerous artifacts to the museum's collection. There is also a 1929 Erie cupola caboose that has been restored with an interior that harkens back to its glory days carrying conductors and engineers.

The museum also has displays of photos depicting the early days of the railroads in Mahwah and a scale model of the Erie system.

With the hustle and bustle of modern living and travel that goes along with it, the old and relaxed travel by train is little but a distant memory that exists only in the minds of an older generation that actually went city-to-city or cross-country east to west or north to south by the Pennsylvania Railroad, the fabled Union Pacific and a host of other lines that today exist only in venues such as this museum.

Train travel was a leisurely way to go. There were glassed-in dome cars where passengers could sit in plush seats and watch the scenery pass by. That was especially alluring when transiting the Rocky Mountains on the way to California.

Other options included a three-day journey from the Northeast to Mexico City with passengers in small private compartments or in a Pullman car, where seats at night were converted into double-decker bunks sealed off by a curtain. Passengers had to climb a ladder to reach the upper bunk and pray they did not have to use the bathroom at night.

The dining car served near-gourmet meals that the railroads considered a loss-leader, making up the difference in the ticket price. Diners sat at tables designed for four people or at a more intimate table for two. All were covered in white linen tablecloths, and food was served by waiters as if in a fine New York restaurant.

The train sped its way southward, and passengers were actually able to see cowboys riding along the prairie, hustling herds of cattle along.

The museum is housed in the original station built in 1871 and was moved to its present site with the building of a new station. Inside is a restored station master's office as it would have appeared during the lifetime of the original station. In addition, artifacts related to the station and the railroad are displayed. Next door is a restored caboose; visitors can enter and view the living and working conditions of the railroad workers.

In 1848, the Paterson and Ramapo Railroad was built and traveled through Mahwah. It was designed to carry passengers and freight from New York City through Paterson to the mainline of the Erie Railroad located in nearby Suffern, New York, literally just over the state border. From that juncture, connections were made to Upstate New York and on to Chicago and the western states.

In 1871, Mahwah petitioned the Erie to permit a stop at a new station in the town. The request was granted, and the new station was in operation until 1904, when the Erie expanded to four tracks and raised the railbed above ground level. A second station was in service until 1914, when it was destroyed by fire. In 1914, the present station was built and remains in service today.

There are docents at both facilities to point out the exhibits and answer questions.

14

OAKLAND

HENDRICK VAN ALLEN HOUSE

George Washington Slept Here…So What Else Is New?

If frequent flier miles were available in the eighteenth century, George Washington would never have had to pay for a place to rest his head or be transported from one location to the next. There's hardly a section of the country that can't boast of myriad locations where the "Traveling George" hasn't slept.

But that also begs the question of whether the founding president actually put his head on a pillow in every location that claims it to be fact. A modern corollary was written by a New York sportswriter when the New York Giants baseball team was on the way to its new digs in San Francisco: "In 20 years if everyone who says he was at the last game in the Polo Grounds was actually there, the Giants would not have had to leave town."

Many locales claim Washington or other major historical figures for the tourist dollars. Jesse James, the notorious bank robber, was shot and killed by one of his own men. Yet numerous towns from Granbury, Texas, to God-knows-where-else claim he was alive and made his home within their borders, later dying a natural death. That proved to be an invention of the local tourist authority.

George Washington truly slept his way around the colonies. He is recorded as having stayed at the Hendrick Van Allen House, now slated to become a museum.

Bergen County today has more places in the National Register of Historic Places than any other county in New Jersey. Battles were fought here. Washington led his troops in skirmishes and his famous retreat here. So it's no surprise that he took succor in numerous buildings to be used as headquarters or sleeping quarters.

One such place confirmed to have hosted the colonial commander-in-chief is Oakland's Hendrick Van Allen House, located only yards away from the Stream House (see page 109) and at the intersection of Ramapo Valley Road (Route 202) and Franklin Avenue, just off I-287.

The home, a Dutch Colonial built by Hendrick Van Allen in 1748, was used by Washington as his B&B and headquarters as he moved his troops from Morristown, New Jersey, to Smith's Clove, New York. He used the building from July 14 to 15 or 16, 1777.

Van Allen and his wife, Elizabeth, lived in the home with their ten children. He was a deacon at the Ponds Church, about one mile west of the home. The structure was of stone masonry with four rooms, large for the period.

Early maps show that Van Allen had built a gristmill across from the home. Ramapo Valley Road, today a tree-lined, curvy roadway leading north toward the New York border, was a main supply route on a north–south line, making it an easy choice for Washington.

Van Allen lived there until his death in July 1783 at the age of seventy-six. The property was then divided among his children. The property subsequently changed hands several times from 1788 to 1864. Records showing ownership for that time are illegible. From 1864 to 1900, the site was owned by three other families, and in 1900, it was taken over by Edward Page, who built the adjacent Stream House.

Washington wrote that he was forced to move his troops over "extremely deep and miry roads," quite unlike the well-paved thoroughfares and highways around the property today.

The Hendrick Van Allen House, built prior to the Revolutionary War, originally occupied hundreds of acres in the town of Oakland. Today it sits just off busy Route 287 on a small parcel of land.

Washington provided documentation that he stayed at Van Allen and used it as his headquarters in letters that he personally wrote.

Bergen County's historic buildings often served multiple purposes over the centuries. In 1778 and 1779, the Van Allen House served as the Bergen County Courthouse.

Edward Day Page, Oakland's second mayor, a dairy farmer and local businessman, later purchased the house as well as about a quarter of what is now Oakland. He held the house in the late nineteenth and early twentieth centuries.

Over time, as the house began to deteriorate from age and neglect, it was saved from demolition by the Oakland Historical Society and help from the Woman's Club of Oakland and preserved as a piece of important local and U.S. history. It now serves as a museum displaying artifacts of colonial Dutch life.

History is of major importance to Bergen County's organizations as well as its governments. The Ramapough Conservancy leased the Van Allen property from Oakland and received a $44,000 grant from the Bergen County Historic Preservation Trust for work on both the Van Allen House and the adjacent Stream House. The Stream House was torn down to the stone foundation and turned into a museum/school around 2022.

The county grant is a drop in the bucket for what is needed to bring the Van Allen House into shape and for work on the Stream House. Estimates range well in excess of $1.5 million.

Plaque detailing Washington's use of the house as his headquarters from July 14 to 17, 1777.

Historic restoration is complex and expensive. It requires approval from both state and county agencies. Once the approvals are obtained, true renovation requires that the buildings be brought back to their original look and state. That involves finding building material that will, as closely as possible, match the original.

Bulldozers were set to enter the picture in 1957, when the property was taken over by the Knoll Top Construction Company with plans to demolish the buildings and erect a gas station. Washington's spirit would have come back to haunt them for those plans.

Former mayor Alexander Potash, who actually lived on the property from 1938 through 1944, urged the borough to purchase and preserve the historic site. In 1966, Oakland took possession of the property, and in 1973, it was added to the State and National Registers of Historic Places.

In 1979, major restoration work was performed in an effort to undo the changes made over the decades and centuries and return it to its original state. In the 1990s and 2000s, several projects undertook these tasks.

With the concern of residents, local government and preservationists, the Van Allen House remains and welcomes visitors.

REVOLUTIONARY WAR BURIAL SITE

Buried for 240 Years and No One Knew Where…

Until November 2021

Too often the dead of various wars lie in unmarked graves on long-forgotten battlefields. To this day, we are still coming across the bodies of soldiers who died in World War II in fields across Europe. The same goes for Korea and in Vietnam. A commission was formed under the direction of Major General Thomas Needham, a decorated former Green Beret, to look for those missing in action (MIA) or those killed in Vietnam and never located.

But imagine being buried for more than 240 years with only rumors and vague memories that you ever existed.

In November 2021, a dedicated group of veterans, members of the American Legion, determined to find out if the rumors were true and, if so, locate the graves of Revolutionary War soldiers.

Following up on leads provided by two and a half centuries of rumor and legend, American Legion Post 369 commander Ronald Beattie led a crew of volunteers through the Pond Cemetery, focusing on a rather large plot in the burial ground that had remained untouched.

The volunteers were supplemented by an infusion of money from a donor who wished to remain anonymous. That opened the door for equipment to be brought in to survey the cemetery and especially the suspected area.

Pond family tradition held that they had donated a portion of land for a cemetery where a restaurant, Portobello, now stands. This proved to be erroneous as the search went on. The actual cemetery fronts well-traveled Ramapo Valley Road. Portobello lies just south of the cemetery. As with so many other locations in Bergen County, there is a connection to George Washington, who is said to have passed this area on his retreat from Saratoga in 1780–81.

It is known that on this trek Washington did stay at the Hendrick Van Allen House a short distance north of the cemetery and on Ramapo Valley Road at the intersection of Route 287. The old house still stands (see page 103) and will be repurposed as a museum.

The cemetery, named for the prominent Ponds family, is adjacent to the Ponds Church, across the street from an ice cream stand and diner and down the block from a popular restaurant. The suspected location of what was thought to be only four bodies was given a thorough survey by electromagnetic equipment obtained through the generosity of the anonymous donor.

The Legionnaires took their time in the search with a desire to do it the right way. The feeling among veterans is something those who are lifelong civilians can never fully understand. The mandate "never leave a brother behind" has no boundaries, no matter how far in the past the conflict may have been. More than that, the suspected remains were those of men who had given their lives in the fight for the formation of this country.

The search went on. Adding strength to the search was the knowledge that Continental soldiers who survived the war and later died are also buried in Ponds Cemetery. But where were the presumed four unidentified soldiers?

Beattie pressed on with the search. After he began the search, Beattie placed three American flags in the suspect area—covering some fifty to sixty yards—each Memorial Day. Such is the loyalty to fallen comrades. Beattie, who served the country as a Marine (never say "former Marine"), was determined to locate the bodies.

The search was all the more difficult because nothing was actually known about those supposedly buried in that plot. Did they die of disease? Of combat wounds?

No known grave markers, if any at all, survived to identify the soldiers or their location. There were no records from the Continental army or the Ponds family. Smiling, Commander Beatie said that they even used divining rods in the search. Diving rods are two sticks held in a *V* pattern with the point facing out and used in search of water. Supposedly, when the pointed end dips down, water is beneath the surface.

Ron Beattie (*right*), commander of the Oakland American Legion Post, along with his post adjutant, salutes marker for the otherwise unmarked grave site of twelve Continental soldiers buried there and undiscovered for more than two centuries.

Marker commemorating the otherwise unmarked burial site. Beattie and his post worked diligently, following rumors of the burial, until they located the actual site.

Finally, the search with the modern equipment began to offer up some resolution. The electromagnetic equipment, ground-penetrating radar, found anomalies in the ground, yielding the probability that bodies were there. But to the surprise of the Legion members, there were not four bodies. Indications were that at least a dozen were buried at the site.

The anonymous donor came through again, and a footstone-style monument was inscribed to honor the memory of those buried there. A small American flag decorates the side of the monument, and red markers delineate the burial site. In mid-November 2021, with the dedication of the monument, the search had come to an end, and those who had given their lives for the formation of what would become the United States of America finally received the respect and honor that had eluded them for nearly two and a half centuries

THE STREAM HOUSE

From Derelict Building to Education Center

Bergen County has long been in the mode of recycling everything from paper goods to plastic. But buildings?

What to do with a historic building that has crumbled well beyond the possibility of rehab to bring it back to what it was in its heyday? That was the problem facing authorities in the borough of Oakland.

A building that once served as an office for a dairy and storage facility had not only outlived its useful purpose but also was little more than a barely standing shell with walls that were falling apart. The entire structure was in danger of collapsing.

The structure, built just after the turn of the twentieth century, didn't have the cachet of the county's historical past that dates to the 1500s, but it stood on hallowed ground adjacent to another building used as a headquarters by George Washington.

Borough officials and historians came up with a solution that seemed to satisfy everyone: tear the remnants of the building down and put up a new edifice in its place that would serve as a museum of the area's long history.

The old dairy office is known locally as the Stream House. That's logical, because it sits atop a small, meandering stream that runs off a busy roadway and not far from a major interstate highway. Some of the building has fallen into the stream and in chunks on the ground adjacent to the old building. Fencing keeps the curious and teens from endangering themselves by entering what can only be described as "derelict." It could have made a terrific location for a Halloween movie.

The Stream House was initially intended to serve as a home for the dairy manager/storage area/office. It would have provided space for the seven-hundred-acre dairy farm owned by then mayor Edward Page. The building was multifunctional, as it also served as Oakland's first library.

As with much farmland close to a nearby metro area, the farm was bought by developers who built a summer residence community following World War II. Developers constructed nearly 1,700 summer homes that were eventually converted to permanent residences.

Local councilman John Biale noted, "Just knocking the Stream House down would have jeopardized any future public consideration." Biale is the council's historic preservation committee's liaison.

One problem confronting the effort is the fact that considerable amounts of asbestos were used to insulate the old building. It was not until recent times that the danger of using asbestos became generally known. Normally, the removal of asbestos requires that it be encapsulated so that fibers are not spread, endangering those in the area.

Once the asbestos removal is accomplished so as not to contaminate the stream and any other environmental concerns addressed, the building will be torn down to its base. The building sits atop what is locally known as Pond Stream, with the water running under it. During the building's early days, that helped keep it and its dairy contents cool.

This picture of the Stream House, sitting only yards from the Hendrick Van Allen House, shows the unfortunate degree of deterioration from both age and neglect. The building sat on a stream that today is only a trickle of water. The house was deemed beyond repair and demolished.

The local government will have to foot the bill for demolition and removal of debris, as there are no grant funds earmarked for tearing a building down. But once that is accomplished, Oakland will be able to apply for grants to construct the new classroom/museum.

Mayor Linda Schwager said she sees a small, one-room museum being built on the site. The mayor envisions an educational center that will complement the adjacent Hendrick Van Allen House (discussed previously) that was built around 1740 and is rich in colonial history.

15

OLD BERGEN THEATERS

Most Bergen County neighborhoods either had a movie theater or there was one close by. Parking was easy, and on weekends especially theaters were inexpensive dates for singles, couples and young married people. Those were the days before the advent of the multiplex theaters with a dozen or more screens; some even offered food service brought to your seats.

Slowly, one by one, neighborhood theaters became a thing of fond memory with only a few refusing to give up the ghost.

Then along came COVID-19, and the doors began to close more rapidly—often with finality. Tenafly lost out; Englewood was a winner.

One of the more popular local theaters, the Tenafly Bow Tie Cinema, was the latest to succumb to the faltering economy. Built in 1926, the theater was popular with patrons from a number of surrounding towns, some of whom had lost their own local theaters in the recent past.

The Bow Tie died a quiet death. It closed when businesses were forced to shut down, and no major announcement of its permanent demise was made. Local officials found out about the loss by accident. The town's mayor was at a chamber of commerce meeting when he found out that the building was listed for sale. The price: $1.395 million.

Governor Phil Murphy ordered theaters to close in order to try to stem the spread of the pandemic. When he permitted them to reopen at a greatly reduced capacity and with social distancing in the auditorium, it was too late. Expenses and overhead had taken their toll, and the iconic theater was about to become history.

Mayor Mark Zinna contacted the representatives at Bow Tie, telling them he would like it to remain a movie theater. Bow Tie did not respond to requests for comment.

The Tenafly Theater opened in the 1920s as an early film house, known as the New Bergen Theatre. It had a small stage, as many early movie houses did, where promotions designed to draw the audience in were often held. The design of the building was classic early movie theater.

Then, some seventy years later, it was obtained by Clearview Cinemas in 1993. In 2013, family-owned Bow Tie purchased the venue. The company is one of the largest theater operators in the country.

Tenafly Bow Tie went dark in 2018 after a feud between the owners and the local government. The borough council was considering a proposal to designate the theater as a historic landmark, an act the owners fought vigorously, fearing it could affect any changes they might later consider with the building.

It had reopened and then shut down again in March 2020 when the governor placed restrictions on public gatherings in an effort to stem the spread of coronavirus.

Since then, various proposals have been made with no final solution as of this writing. Mayor Mark Zinna expressed the hope that it could remain a movie theater, but alternative proposals abound. He said the borough would consider purchasing the building and leasing it back as a theater. The borough has already done something similar with the former Tenafly Railroad Station on Piermont Road.

Zinna said he would welcome either a theater or an art venue, something that would mesh well with the lifestyle of Tenafly. He also suggested the possibility of producing live theater.

The local chamber of commerce chimed in when its president, Christine Evron, supported Zinna. She went a step further, suggesting the borough purchase the property and consider turning it into a nightclub. The theater is soundproofed, and the festivities in a club would not affect surrounding stores.

A liquor license, critical to the operation of a nightclub, would not be a problem, as it would not be limited by Tenafly's license limits.

The problems faced by small and historic theaters such as the Bow Tie have also affected some of the major chains. AMC theaters rents an auditorium for private gatherings for a pittance, ninety-nine dollars.

In Englewood, the Bergen Performing Arts Center (Bergen PAC) first opened in November 1926 as the Englewood Plaza Movie Theater. As in Tenafly, the movie house was popular with locals and visitors.

In 1967, the theater was purchased by United Artists, a consortium of movie stars, and remained open through 1973. It stood vacant for years until a small group of theater aficionados along with concert impresario John Harms revitalized the venue.

Harms led a drive in the late 1970s to revitalize, restore and preserve the Englewood Plaza Theater as a venue for live performances. To this day, above the marquee his name is enshrined in the concrete façade. The theater was named for him: the John Harms Performing Arts Center. He managed to preserve the vintage and historic acoustics of the building.

Although it was one of the larger such venues in New Jersey, it closed on April 14, 2003. But the old theater had the lives of a cat. A mere sixteen days later, it was reincarnated as Bergen PAC gratis of a small but determined public-private partnership. One of the main proponents of the project was then mayor Frank Huttle III, who lent his personal support as well as that of the City of Englewood.

The theater reopened in the fall of 2004 boasting 1,367 seats in the Old Grande Dame. Considered by most to be a theater of historic relevance, Bergen PAC offered a state-of-the-art recording studio.

To the delight of theatergoers from all over the region, Bergen PAC has presented the likes of well-known television star and comedian Jay Leno; rockers Dee Snider and Bo Bice; Blood, Sweat & Tears, Chris Daughtry; Amy Poehler; Tina Fey; and Melissa McCarthy.

During the pandemic, the theater hosted outdoor concerts and made preparations to return to the stage as soon as feasible. When the masks are gone, the show will go on.

16

ORADELL

THE LITTLE FIREHOUSE THEATER

Bergen County Players Bring Joy to a New Generation

What do you do with an old firehouse that is of no use and can't hold more modern equipment? The bells don't clang any more. There's no more rushing of men jumping into protective gear, but there are appreciative audiences piling into a repurposed old firehouse, now home to the Bergen County Players and the Little Firehouse Theater.

In 1897, the first volunteer fire department in Oradell was organized. The local government moved quickly to accommodate their needs and voted to provide a hand-pulled hose cart and seven hundred feet of hose. Shortly after that, a horse-drawn hook and ladder was purchased.

The timing was fortuitous, as days after the department was formed and equipped, a major fire broke out nearby. Alarms calling the firefighters to action were a far cry from today. The bell in the tower of the Reformed Church pealed as a summons.

To upgrade the alarm system, several locomotive wheel rims were purchased and set up in various locations. They were "activated" by a series of hammer blows that rang out loud enough for the volunteers to hear. One of these antique devices is still on public view in front of the modern firehouse on Kinderkamack Road. That alarm system was in use until 1912, when a system of "toots" was set up with a whistle at the waterworks in neighboring New Milford.

Right: The modern Bergen County Players venue in an old firehouse. The players put on regular shows that have become popular throughout the country.

Opposite: An 1897 view of the firehouse in its original use with the Oradell Volunteer Firemen arrayed outside with some of their equipment.

Realizing the need for a headquarters and a place to store the equipment when not in use, the town authorized construction of a firehouse, now the home of the Bergen County Players. Eventually, the hand-drawn hose cart was replaced by a modern (by standards of the day) horse-drawn hose cart. In 1916, motorized equipment replaced the "hay burner," with additional vehicles coming the following year.

The volunteer firemen were sufficiently adept at their jobs that there is no record of serious injury or death, with the exception of the odd cow or horse over the years in a barn fire.

Oradell was and is an upscale white-collar community with a passion for the arts. In the early 1900s, several amateur theater groups were formed. One aimed its talents at Camp Merritt in Cresskill, where soldiers were stationed in a holding pattern before being sent into combat overseas. Several original productions were performed to entertain the troops and keep them occupied.

The local actors also put on shows as fundraisers for the borough and other organizations. Over time, the reputations of these theater groups grew in stature.

In 1932, with the Great Depression raging, the theater groups aimed to take people's minds off the country's problems. Productions were presented throughout Bergen County. The groups met in a wide variety of venues, including barns and one with a pot-bellied stove. Part of the "audience" included a family of skunks living in the basement. There are no reports of the skunks expressing their views of the productions.

In the winter of 1944, possibly caused by that stove, the building burned to the ground. No one is sure exactly how the fire started, but it did start the players on a search for a new and permanent home.

In the true theater tradition, the show went on, opening on schedule in the auditorium of what was then Bergen Junior College. Today, it is known as Fairleigh Dickinson University.

Looking to go a step beyond, a group met in the old Hackensack Y and approved a charter forming the Bergen County Players organization. Among those charter members was Helen Burke Travolta, mother of future movie and television star John Travolta.

Fortune was about to take a turn for the positive. In 1949, Oradell approved the construction of a new and modern firehouse. That move left the old 1897 fire headquarters redundant. It remained vacant.

The Bergen County Players had a vision and opened negotiations with the town to take over the space and create a theater, giving the group a permanent home.

Rolling up their sleeves, the Bergen County Players built a stage in the rear of the building and installed seats in place of the old firefighting equipment. Some years later, the group built an extension to what became known as the Little Firehouse Theater. It increased seating capacity to more than two hundred, upgraded to an electric lightboard in 1980, installed central air-conditioning in 1982, computerized the box office in the 1990s and then made the theater accessible to those with disabilities, among other and ongoing improvements.

Becoming more a part of Oradell and the surrounding community, Bergen County Players developed a series called Conversations with an Artist in order to provide members of the public with an opportunity to engage in conversation with professional artists.

Each season, Bergen County Players features seven main stage and at least two secondary stage presentations. In December, children are the focus with a production aimed toward the young.

Today, the nonprofit Bergen County Players boasts some three hundred member-volunteers. The organization boasts that it is a family and points to the fact that a number of married couples first met while volunteering at the Little Firehouse Theater. And that was without a production of either *The Bachelor* or *The Bachelorette*.

As a result of the quality of its productions, the Little Firehouse Theater has been host to many well-known professional actors who have stepped on the boards either as they were on the way up or even after they've made it.

Some of the names you might recognize are: New Milford's Rob McClure, who starred on Broadway in *Chaplin*, *Something Rotten!* and *Noises Off* and *Mrs. Doubtfire*, among other productions; Robert Sean Leonard, an Emmy Award winner for his role in television's *House*; and Beth Fowler of *Sweeney Todd*. Bergen County resident and famed best-selling mystery author Mary Higgins Clark appeared as well.

In their eighty-five-plus-year history, Bergen County Players and the Little Firehouse Theater have set a standard for community theaters around the country. At the same time, there is a reverence for the history of the building they now occupy.

COOL BEANS

Hottest Spot in Town Was "Cool"

Hip, straight, bent, nobody paid any attention. Coffee or a light snack or just hang out…that was the setting for River Edge's coffeehouse, Cool Beans, like a hippie haven west of Greenwich Village.

A grungy little hangout stuffed between the Little Firehouse Theater and a market, Cool Beans was loved by its regulars and even those who just stopped by to soak in the atmosphere. There were couches, stuffed chairs and wooden seats, and all were usually filled by a loyal clientele.

Outsiders were never made to feel like outsiders. Regulars had their favorite seats, but should an outsider take up residence there, so what? It was never a problem.

Cool Beans served a variety of smooth coffees and other libations. There were even snacks. The atmosphere was almost that of a small community center. People sat around sipping their drinks while others chatted and some read magazines, books or newspapers. There were patrons in shorts (depending on the weather), raggedy jeans and suits with white shirts and ties. No one ever got a sideways glance.

Then progress happened. Cool Beans entered history and is about to become an upscale restaurant and banquet hall. The restaurant would seat some 240 people, about 200 more than Cool Beans could accommodate. The front is planned to take on a more modern, glassed-in look, and there will be outdoor dining and even a vegetable garden.

From a single-story coffeehouse, the proposed edifice will rise to two stories and offer valet parking, requiring removal of two curbside parking spaces. No off-street parking is planned for its location on perpetually busy Kinderkamack Road.

Of the 248 seats in the new eatery, 128 will be on the first floor. There will be an additional 28 seats in a patio in front of the building. The upper level will offer seating for 125 diners.

This poses an interesting situation. As mentioned, the restaurant/catering hall is planned to have 248 seats, but the math does not add up. The sum of first and second floors as announced total 253 seats. That does not include the front patio with an announced 28 seats for an overall total of 281.

If the local government approves the removal of the two curbside parking spots, the new owners plan to have the cars being valeted parked in a public lot on the west side of Kinderkamack Road behind the public library.

Now closed coffeeshop Cool Beans was something out of New York's Greenwich Village. People relaxed, hippies and businesspeople gathered and no one felt out of place. It will be demolished to make way for a large restaurant.

Use of a patio would not alter the site in any major form, as there currently is one in the rear. The present building covers 8,600 square feet and would be replaced with a 10,400-square-foot edifice.

It could benefit from its location adjacent to the Old Firehouse, home to the Bergen County Players community theater. Remaining would be Anthony's Oradell Prime Meat Market, which is expected to remain where it is.

Some Oradell residents are concerned about noise, parking and the imminent loss of another historic building.

As of this writing, Cool Beans has been demolished down to the ground with a new foundation already in place.

BLAUVELT MANSION

Historic House or Another Nursing Home?

The huge structure—looking much like a castle out of a Harry Potter movie—sits eerily atop a hill overlooking a roadway busy with traffic, watching, waiting, a mysterious entity that should not be messed with.

But the unfortunate truth is that there appears to be an attempt to do away with what is known today as the Blauvelt Mansion in the town of Oradell, which overlooks a centuries-old roadway once used as an Indian trail, Kinderkamack Road.

With the Dutch influence permeating Bergen County, it's normal for many people to assume the road's name has a base in Holland. They'd be wrong. The mansion's address goes back to the Lenape people who populated much of northeastern New Jersey prior to the European invasion.

The common assumption that the Dutch word for "children," *kinder*, had something to do with the name was understandable. But those who delve into the history of the area would fnd that the original name of what was then a dirt roadway was Kintekaye Ack or, in Lenape, "Place of Council." The tribes held sessions there to discuss and determine courses of action and other more mundane issues. They would hold ceremonial dances and prayer sessions.

Many Indigenous names and designations have been corrupted over the course of years and centuries. Several names found their way along this road until it was finally designated Kinderkamack Road.

Before the mansion was built, the property was owned by Richard and Euphemia Van Wagoner. They built a Dutch Colonial–style home

The Blauvelt Mansion sits atop a hill overlooking Kinderkamack Road. The lion is visible in front, seemingly protecting the mansion from historically challenged developers.

constructed of sandstone. Their tenancy predated the Revolution. In 1895, they sold the property to Kimball Chase Atwood. Atwood was somewhat of a financial mogul as the founder of an insurance company and grapefruit magnate.

In 1897, Atwood built the mansion that today looms over Kinderkamack Road. In the late seventeenth century, the site was part of a 261-acre estate owned by Andres Tebow, an immigrant from the European Low Countries. While games that were played by children and adults of that era would be unrecognizable today, our sports would be the same to them. Move up perhaps ten generations from the time old Andres Tebow moved in, and he would not recognize what his descendant Tim Tebow, the former NFL quarterback, was doing throwing an odd-shaped ball across a field.

The twenty-five-room mansion sits on a huge front lawn that slopes down to Kinderkamack Road. Its large foundation, steep-pitched gable roof, hexagonal towers and conical roof have made the building a landmark for generations. The original Dutch Colonial home built by Andres Tebow was demolished in 1892.

Atwood spent $100,000, then a massive amount of money, on the construction. And that did not take into account the cost of the outbuildings. He then christened the home Northland.

Atwood owned the property until 1926, when he sold it to Elmer Blauvelt, who rechristened it Bluefield. In old English, Blauvelt means "blue field."

Along with his son, Hiram Bellis Demarest Blauvelt (who died in modern times in 1957), Elmer owned a coal and lumber business Theirs is among the names that continually appear in the history of Bergen County.

Young Hiram served in Africa in World War II and was an avid hunter. Currently, his collections of mounted animals and wildlife art are displayed adjacent to the mansion in what was originally the carriage house and today is the Hiram Blauvelt Art Museum and Foundation. It is open to the public on a limited basis. Hiram, a philanthropist, had hoped to promote the cultural value of wildlife and the conservation of such animals—an interesting concept in view of the fact that he killed so many of them for display.

After Hiram's passing, his mother, Margaret Bellis Blauvelt (d. 1961), held ownership. Unfortunately, the building was inhabited only by caretakers who did little caretaking. It was slated for demolition until it was sold to architect Raymond Wells in 1978. Wells, who had a sense of history and appreciation for design and architecture, halted any demolition plans, renovated the building and used it for his residence and offices.

Carriage house adjacent to the Blauvelt Mansion.

Artwork, such as the majestic lion sculpture, adorns the grounds of the Blauvelt Mansion.

Upkeep and maintenance of the huge building was considerable, and it was listed for sale in 2006. Experiencing financial difficulties, the Wells family approached the local government in Oradell and requested help in saving the mansion. Nothing came of that, and in 2013, the mansion was sold at a sheriff's auction, after having gone into foreclosure.

It was purchased by CareOne, a nursing home and assisted living corporation with a facility directly across Kinderkamack Road on the east side facing the mansion. Since 2007, the corporation had been attempting to build an assisted living facility. With the purchase, the plan was to demolish the mansion and put up a brick and mortar building in place of the historic structure.

CareOne has been charged by some with permitting the property to deteriorate to a point where it would be unsalvageable. The feeling in Oradell and by preservationists is that by letting the mansion degrade to a point where restoration would be costly and difficult, CareOne would seek permission to demolish the mansion and replace the historic structure with a modern healthcare facility. CareOne has remained largely silent. Efforts to obtain comment from CareOne for this book received no response to several telephone calls.

That plan ran into serious opposition from the Oradell Planning Board, before which the organization is required to apply and obtain approval for any construction. Opposition to CareOne's plan ran into a wall of opposition from Oradell residents, who revere the historic building. Preservationists in Bergen County joined in as well.

Having lost so much history and heritage to bulldozers and residential and commercial developers, many Bergen County residents took up the cudgels of preserving what was left. Today, of the original buildings on the site, only the mansion and carriage house with the museum remain.

The loss of the building would be a dagger to the heart of Bergen County's history. In 1941, a local county publication called the mansion "the most imposing home in the Hackensack valley."

As of this writing, (Atwood) Blauvelt Mansion and the museum in the carriage house have been holding on. But for how long that can be maintained is another question. If they are left to continue to deteriorate, there may be little choice but to add another piece of Bergen County's history to the reference books.

Preservationists reported that there may be holes in the roof and ceiling and that animals such as racoons have taken up residence in the structure.

NEW JERSEY'S SPACE PIONEER

New Jersey can boast of many achievements in the arts and sciences, perhaps more than most other states. But a record that can't be topped is the fact that two of its natives racked up achievements in space. Nearby Essex County's proud native son Edwin "Buzz" Aldrin, a former fighter pilot who was on three space missions, made history as the second human being to walk on the moon as a crew member on the Apollo 11 mission.

Bergen County's space hero was an Oradell native who was one of the original American astronauts and a participant in the Mercury 7 adventures. He named his capsule Sigma 7.

Walter "Wally" Schirra, a World War II fighter pilot, was chosen for the first class of American astronauts working to fulfill John F. Kennedy's promise that an American would walk on the moon before the decade of the 1960s was over. JFK didn't live to see that, and Schirra never made it to the moon. But he was an integral part of the lead-up to the Apollo 11, which brought Aldrin and Neil Armstrong to the lunar surface and into the history books.

But as with any major scientific stride, it took many steps to reach that point, and Schirra was a major part of the effort. The former Navy fighter pilot, who died on May 3, 2007, was the only astronaut to

Left: Gazebo in Schirra Park.

Right: Plaque honoring Oradell native Commander Walter "Wally" Schirra as the "First Jerseyan to go into space." He did six orbits in Sigma 7 on October 3, 1962, spending nine hours in space.

reach space in three programs: Mercury, Gemini and Apollo.

Today at a small park at the intersection of Kinderkamack Road and Oradell Avenue, a blue plaque with white lettering notes that "the First Jerseyan to Walk in Space" came from this borough. And while that is the only marker commemorating Schirra, he remains a major source of pride to the community.

Temporary design on paths honoring astronaut Wally Schirra.

Artist Nina Tsur from neighboring New Milford said she was surprised to learn that someone from the next town over had done so much. As an artist, she determined to do more.

At her suggestion, the walkways in the park across from the post office would become a mural to honor Schirra. And while most murals simply hang from a museum wall or decorate passing trains, trucks and building walls courtesy of vandals, Tsur's would be interactive, permitting visitors to walk through and admire the work.

Playing on the name of the Where's Wally? series, Tsur gave the project the same name, noting that few called Schirra "Walter." He was known to all as "Wally."

The artwork covers some 2,250 feet of the walkways on the village green; there are images of Wally in astronaut gear and space icons. There are also a few faux Wallys designed to throw people off the trail.

Schirra, born in 1923, was the son of a World War I pilot. Wally's parents were extraordinary for the time, and he could see how daring they were.

After the war, his father, Walter Sr., became a barnstorming pilot, performing across the country. His mother, Florence, was hardly a wallflower. She participated in Walter Sr.'s aerial shows as a wing-walker, an exceptionally dangerous activity, but designed to wow the crowds of paying onlookers.

Young Wally graduated from the U.S. Naval Academy at Annapolis in 1945 and rapidly distinguished himself in combat, earning three Distinguished Flying Cross medals. During the Korean conflict, he switched service branches and saw more combat as an Air Force pilot.

As an astronaut, Schirra was selected to pilot the Gemini 6A mission in 1965. He met up with Gemini 7 in an exercise designed to prepare for space rendezvous in future missions leading to the moon landing. He moved his spacecraft to within one foot of Gemini 7 and held it in place for several hours. He later became the first person of any nation to ride into space three times when he was assigned to Apollo 7.

Visitors can see and walk through the *Where's Wally* mural at their leisure. But they are cautioned to hurry, as it is not intended to be a permanent artistic display.

17

PARAMUS

BERGEN MUSEUM

The Bergen County Museum of Art and Science closed its doors in 2010 when it lost its space in the Bergen Mall, a major shopping center in Paramus. When it had a physical venue, this privately owned and run museum displayed a quality art collection as well as two Ice Age mastodons that were found and excavated in Bergen County. It is a loss for us all that the museum and its collections will no longer be available for our viewing. Unfortunately, through a lack of interest, the Bergen County Museum of Art and Science has joined the list of assets "Going...Going...Gone."

HARMON VAN DIEN HOUSE

Along Paramus Road stands the Harmon Van Dien House, currently a private residence. It is listed in the National Register of Historic Places as probably built by Harmon Van Dien. The date attributed to its construction is 1811. Speculation on the date of construction is attributed to a date painted on a beam in the cellar.

Coauthor Howard Cohn was fortunate to be able to visit and photograph the main building and smokehouse. Much of the original building remains and displays the construction features of an eighteenth- or nineteenth-century house. The use of mortise and tenon joints connecting beams is evident throughout the building.

In the cellar, one can view the brick arches serving as firming supports for the fireplaces and chimneys within the house. The painted "1811" is also easily found. Although that year is used by some for dating the construction, parts may be older. The Zabriskie family possessed this land earlier and undoubtedly built structures on it in the eighteenth century that were ultimately replaced.

According to local lore, there were buildings on both sides of Paramus Road during the Revolutionary War. The smokehouse/kitchen behind the Van Dien House had a chimney that has since been removed. It was used to bake bread for both the Continental army and the British, depending on who was controlling the area at the time.

Oral history indicates that under British control, the smokehouse was left standing to supply bread for their troops, while the building across the road was burned down because of the residents' support for the Revolution. The grave of Harmon (spelled Herman on the marker) and members of his family can be found in the Valleau Cemetery of the Old Paramus Reformed Church in Ridgewood.

LUTKINS-HOPPER-NEARING HOUSE

Sometimes History Trumps the Bulldozers

"I heard something about that, but no one has told me anything" commented a young man standing among hanging flowerpots, shrubs and a score of garden ornaments at the Northern Border Tree Farm & Nursery on East Ridgewood Avenue and Paramus Road.

The young man was the sole employee at the nursery, setting up displays and handling all sales. But he had no idea if he would be employed for long or if the nursery would become part of history.

Asked about the historic Lutkins-Hopper-Nearing House on the south side of the property, he said he had no idea what the building was, if it was part of the nursery property or if it would be moved or demolished.

Developers had apparently purchased the property that included the nursery, the adjacent Lutkins House on the south side of the property abutting the nursery and a building called the Mill House on the northern edge of the property.

Paramus had granted permits for the demolition of the nursery and the adjacent Mill House, deeming it of no true historic value. Plans for the property are to build a commercial building.

That property once served as a gristmill with water power provided by the flowing Saddle River. Over time, the river moved in a different direction, leaving the mill without a source of power. The mill has been lost to history, but the adjacent building remains. The builders contend that structure is of no historic importance as a result of physical changes.

While the remainder of the property will go to that Memory Garden in the Sky, the Lutkins-Hopper-Nearing House is slated to be moved to another location and preserved. Where that location may be was not determined at the time of this writing. The new location may not be a major move. Discussions appear to indicate that it will be located elsewhere on the property near where it now stands.

That being said, preservationists and local history buffs have expressed concern that at the age of the house, such a move to a new location could be a disaster. They are asking for assurances that when the structure is lifted and prepared for such a move it will not simply collapse.

Tim Adriance, a county historian and longtime advocate for preserving historical properties in Bergen County, has asked that Paramus require a "significant bond" to ensure that the move is undertaken in such a manner that the building will arrive at its new location in one piece.

Adriance also commented that if it means saving only one structure, the Lutkins House or the Mill House, he would save the Lutkins property. That building is a Jersey Dutch design with Federal detailing dating to the late eighteenth century and is only one of a handful of such houses remaining in the county.

Peter Primavera, a historian involved with a historic preservation firm hired by the developer, A2 Enterprises LLC, declared that the Mill House is of no historic significance after studying the properties. He concluded that the Mill House had originally been a barn. Primavera noted that it had been renovated and lost any importance. He contended that the interior of the building had been "obliterated" and remodeled into a house in the 1920s.

Lending historic cachet to the Lutkins House, the Paramus Master Plan included it in a list of historic properties in the borough. As of this writing, the buildings remain but the nursery has been closed.

OLD RED MILL AND THE EASTON TOWER

In its earliest days, Bergen County was mainly an agrarian-based culture and economy.

Today, Paramus is densely populated and home to arguably more shopping malls than any other location in the United States. The late Joe Delaney, Paramus police chief, once quipped: "Paramus is the Indian name for shopping center."

But in the early days, farms abounded throughout the area, with many producing grains as their major crop.

But what to do with all that grain once harvested? It didn't make sense for every farm or community to have a mill rather than a handful located within easy distance of the fields. There was also the need for a power source, and Bergen County was blessed with a number of streams and rivers powerful enough to spin a water wheel that powered an interior grindstone.

Of the many mills in Bergen County, only one remains standing. The wheel is still standing, although it no longer moves, and the waters of the Saddle River move much slower. But the Old Red Mill is still a connection to our beginnings.

Or not.

There is information that the original Red Mill fell into severe disrepair in the 1800s and was ultimately demolished in 1894. There are other reports that it is still in existence, and some mistake the Easton Tower for the mill. If it is still there, it must be invisible.

While the mill once stood on open ground along the stream, today it is bounded by busy Route 4, Saddle River Road, Paramus Road and the Red Mill Road. Drive by too fast, and you'll miss the turnoff. Alongside the road is a historical marker commemorating the structure and its history.

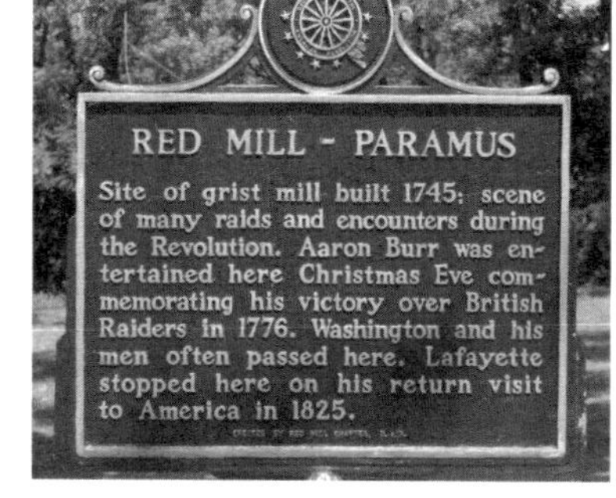

Descriptive plaque for the famed Old Red Mill that entertained Washington (of course), Aaron Burr, the Marquis de Lafayette and a host of other founding fathers.

The gristmill was built in 1745 and later acquired by Jacob Zabriskie, who leased eighty acres around the mill area in 1776. In 1771, he took ownership of the mill. Aside from grinding wheat and grains, the mill had a fairly memorable history. Early maps identify it as the Demarest and Zabriskie Mills, although

The Old Red Mill, no longer red and no longer a mill. The water that once ran beneath it and powered the water wheel is now a slight trickle unable to power anything. But it is a regular stop for many residents and area visitors.

only Jacob Zabriskie appears to have been connected to the structure. That might have been as a result of Jacob Zabriskie's prominence in the county. He was a Bergen County freeholder.

The title *freeholder* stood until 2020, when counties opted to change to the more modern term *county commissioner*. A freeholder was a designation afforded to any White male who was free of debt and owned unencumbered land, thus a "freeholder."

During the Revolution, it was a hot combat zone between Patriots and British forces. On Christmas Eve 1776, Aaron Burr was entertained near the site to commemorate his victory over British raiders.

George Washington, who seemingly never missed any location in the colonies during the war, came by with his troops. Marie-Joseph Paul Yves Roch Gilbert du Motier, better known in the colonies simply as the Marquis de Lafayette, who served as a general in the Revolutionary War, stopped at the mill site on his return to America in 1825. He had developed a close relationship with Washington, Alexander Hamilton and other notables during the Revolution. The Frenchman made what could be considered a victory tour of the then twenty-four United States from August 16, 1824, to September 7, 1825. He actually visited all twenty-four states on this historic visit.

Although born and bred a Frenchman, Lafayette followed the family tradition of militarism. He was commissioned an officer in the French army at the incredible age of thirteen. In America, he was made a general in the Continental army at nineteen. For his service in the Revolution, Lafayette was forever welcomed and remembered in this country. American troops in World War I, on entering France, would shout, "Lafayette we are here."

The mill earned its designation as the Old Red Mill in the early 1800s under the then ownership of Albert Westervelt, who had it painted it the distinctive color.

Near where the mill once stood is another site, the Easton Tower, often mistaken for the mill. Built in the 1700s, the tower also stands along the Saddle River. The Easton Tower was owned by Edward D. Easton, who bought a forty-eight-acre site that contained the mill. The area was known as Arcola. The name was suggested by Easton's father, who brought the family there and named the area for a town in Italy.

Easton was quite the figure. Born in 1856, he died in 1915, but not before he made major contributions to technology. He started life as a stenographer and reporter, later becoming a court stenographer in Washington, D.C. There he covered a number of notable trials throughout the 1880s. He obtained a patent in 1886 when he developed a method of engraving wax cylinders, enabling them to reproduce sound. He founded and became president of the Columbia Phonograph Company, which ultimately became one of the major recording companies in the early twentieth century.

The borough's name comes from the original inhabitants of the area, the Lenni Lenape. The name came from the Lenape word *peramsepuss*, which translates to "land of the wild turkeys." Or it might have been "the fertile fields where turkeys are found." Today, in one of the major shopping malls, Paramus Park, a rather large metal statue of a wild turkey is on display.

VAN DIEN-RUFFGARTEN HOUSE

Bulldozers Set to Take Down Another Historic Home?

Cut down enough trees, and the forest will disappear, as will any chance to clean the air and make oxygen.

Bulldoze enough historic buildings, and our past will disappear.

New Jersey, and Bergen County in particular, has a sense of history and preservation. But that doesn't mean that houses that go back in our history have not been demolished because they were left to rot or developers have eyed the property to build expensive subdivisions.

In some instances, bulldozers suddenly appeared in the early morning and took down historic buildings before anyone could put a stop to the desecration.

Such is the questionable fate of the more-than-180-year-old Van Dien–Ruffgarten House in Paramus, home to more malls and shopping centers than few others places in this country. With builders searching the popular borough, it's not hard to understand why they might be looking with coveting eyes at a nine-acre plot they consider ripe for development.

Known locally, but incorrectly, as the "Mud House," the Van Dien House is, in fact, one of only six remaining examples in Paramus of a Jersey Dutch Stone House.

The historic house, built around 1840, is an ever increasingly rare example of old buildings constructed mostly or entirely of stone. Early settlers used the method because of the abundance of such building material; stone was plentiful, inexpensive and created a sturdy home that would withstand the elements for generations.

The Van Dien–Ruffgarten structure was mislabeled a "mud house" in the 1960s by a local historian not familiar with this method of construction. That might come under the heading of "if you don't know, just say something, anything." This misnomer was not uncommon, as self-styled historians with good intentions sought to label and preserve history. No harm was done except to the purists and aesthetics of the house.

That being said, the "historian" could be forgiven for the error, as the method of building *was* to place the stones in a mortar made of mud. When dried, it would hold the stone in place much the same as true mortar. China's Great Wall was constructed with a similar method, using mud mixed with rice and straw. And it is still standing in most sections and has been for nearly a millennium.

As the name notes, the home was built by the well-to-do Van Dien family and is believed to be one of the last Jersey Dutch Stone Houses built.

However, interestingly, local census records seem to indicate that the home was occupied several years later, in the 1850s through the 1860s, by African families. They were a segment of a small group of both independent and educated folks later designated as African Americans. The group was known to have been living in the area at the time.

By the end of the 1860s, the house had been sold to Peter Ruffgarten, who had recently come to America from the Netherlands. Ruffgarten then enlarged the one-room structure, adding a framed section.

In more modern times, the home was used as a boardinghouse. Today it is uninhabitable and seriously deteriorated.

The Paramus Historic Preservation Society has attempted to save the building, asking the borough governing body to consider purchasing it. In a tight financial economy, the borough council demurred. Paramus is rather densely populated with huge tracts of commercial property and malls. That makes this nine-acre tract exceptionally desirable to builders. This is evidenced by the fact that another piece of property nearby, considerably smaller than the Van Dien-Ruffgarten property, was sold and redeveloped with twenty town houses.

WASHINGTON SPRING

Cooled George, Lafayette and Continental Troops

There are arguably more places George Washington stopped, slept, ate and took respite during the hard days of the American Revolution than spots in which he did not make an appearance.

Washington Spring in Van Saun County Park. Washington's troops encamped near here because of the clear waters of the spring. Washington and Lafayette also visited.

Washington Spring in Paramus's Van Saun County Park is one that can be added to the list of "George Washington stopped here."

Today the site is probably close to the bucolic setting Washington saw during his respite there. The spring is little more than a trickle, worn down by the ravages of time and silt, but it still flows north to south.

A small bridge spans the narrow little creek, offering visitors the opportunity to stand midstream and envision the general astride his white horse as the steed dipped his head to partake of the then clear, flowing waters.

The date was September 4, 1780, as Washington shepherded his weary troops to an encampment in what is now Van Saun County Park. His fourteen thousand troops had moved into a strategic encampment west of the Hackensack River between Newbridge to the south and Kinderkamack in the north. Just north was the hamlet of Steenrapie, known today as the borough of River Edge.

Local farmer Hendrick Banta, part of the family that colonized much of Bergen County, is reported to have sold a barrel of cider to the troops every other day. Banta's ten-year-old son, Cornelius, told his father, and apparently others as well, that on at least three occasions he saw George Washington at the spring and on one instance saw him watering his horse.

It is known that the Marquis de Lafayette was in that area at the same time, and unconfirmed reports place the two of them jointly at the spring.

On September 17, 1780, Washington and Lafayette headquartered in the northern end of the large encampment in an area today called Soldier Hill Road in the borough of Oradell, leading east to west. Around that time, Washington and Lafayette left the area on their way to Connecticut.

Their plan was to meet up with commanding officers of the French army to aid the Continentals. Washington's troops remained in the Paramus/Oradell/River Edge area until September 20, 1780, when they decamped and moved on.

Visitors today to Washington Spring find a beautifully landscaped area that provides a serene spot to sit and relax. There is a winding path leading from the main roadway in the park to the spring. There are curved areas with stone benches for visitors. On any given day, these seats are often taken by parkgoers sitting and reading or just relaxing.

There is a plaque by the spring detailing its history. Another plaque has been placed by the roadway at the entry point to the path leading to the spring.

ZABRISKIE MAUSOLEUM

A Golf Course Hazard?

Golf courses have water hazards, bunkers and rough patches, but how many have a mausoleum?

The Paramus Public Golf Course is located on land that was once part of the vast holdings of the Zabriskie family. A portion of this land originally was used as a cemetery. There are currently two remnants evidencing this prior use. They appear to date from the eighteenth century.

Near fairway 12 stand the remains of a mausoleum constructed of artistically carved native sandstone, set in an impressive mound. It originally had the capacity to hold the remains of twenty-four family members in above-ground partitions. The roof and portions of the sidewalls have since collapsed, as well as almost all of the internal divisions.

The overgrowth of weeds hides much of what is left to the viewer. The original doors and gates have long since disappeared, but what remains of the façade gives one the impression of how beautiful it once was.

Nearby on fairway 13, one cannot miss a much smaller arched burial vault, built into the side of a small hill. The entrance doors to this vault no

The Zabriskie mausoleum, now an empty shell except for debris piled in it. The bodies were long ago moved and reinterred.

longer exist, but inside one easily sees where the bodies rested. Six bodies were able to be interred here, along two levels. The surrounding areas were also used as a cemetery, but any other vaults are no longer apparent.

In 1922, the remains still contained in these two sites were reinterred in the Valleau Cemetery belonging to the Old Paramus Church in Ridgewood. They joined other family members buried nearby. A stone was erected over their final resting place and simply engraved: "Zabriskie Bodies Taken from Guilliam Zabriskie Vault."

ZABRISKIE-TENANT HOUSE

Going…Going…Gone

The borough of Paramus is so exceptionally rich in the history of the nascent United States. Washington and many of the most prominent figures in the Revolution and years after passed through. The early Dutch settlers left their imprint on roads, towns and historic sites.

What is little known is that Bergen County had a dark side to its history. While states to the south were known for their slaveholdings, most county residents to this day have no idea that slavery was alive and well in the county. And that is despite the fact that there are signs and evidence throughout the county. There are several cemeteries devoted to both free people of color and those who died still in bondage.

In a rare show of unity between descendants of those who enslaved and those who suffered, both sides came together in what turned out to be a futile effort to save a home tied to Bergen County slaves.

The Zabriskie-Tenant House, a rare example of Dutch sandstone architecture that was located at 273 Dunkerhook Road, was turned into a pile of rubble when a developer refused efforts to preserve it and turn the old building into a museum.

The home had served as a dwelling for the Zabriskie family, one of the more prominent settlers in the region. Interestingly, it also was home to the Bennett and Stewart families, descendants of slaves who built the structure in 1790.

Without advance notice or warning, a backhoe was brought to the site by Quattro 4, an LLC that controlled the property. By the time the backhoe was finished the next morning, the Zabriskie-Tenant House was little more than a pile of rubble and fond memories, exasperating the preservationist group interested in the building. The only part of the structure that remained was a staircase that once led to the entrance.

Nearby Bergen Community College, one of the more prominent and community-minded organizations, had offered to move the structure to its extensive campus, where it could be upgraded and converted to a museum, according to Darryl Harris, a descendant of Samuel Bennett, one of the slaves who had lived in the home.

Harris, a Paterson resident, said that a grant had been applied for and was about to be approved when the situation became moot because of the destruction. "Today we found out that the house had just been knocked down." Harris said that the developer's lawyer claimed he did not know the house was slated to be demolished.

18

RAMSEY

THE OLD STONE HOUSE

Just another old stone building? Hardly. The borough's Old Stone House, sitting atop what might generously be described as a "bluff," has a history going back to the eighteenth century and served as everything from a tavern to an antique store to a private home. Today it serves the Ramsey Historical Society as a museum, open to the public on rare occasions.

The Old Stone House's history, while documented, leaves some open questions. Part of a three-hundred-acre-farm, it was originally built sometime around 1746, possibly by Jan Westervelt, one of the pioneering families of Bergen County. The land is believed to have been leased to Uriah and Ruloff Westervelt in or around 1744 and was a portion of the Ramapough Tract (named for the local tribe). According to the Ramsey Historical Society (RHS), it was held by Peter Fauconier, one of the original purchasers.

The tract is located between the Ramapough Mountains and the Saddle River and was purchased from the Indian tribe on November 18, 1709. It was then owned by the Westervelts through the early part of the 1800s and was sold to others in 1837.

From 1837 through 1955, the property changed hands several times until it was taken over by the State of New Jersey. Controversy erupted when the state transportation authority took ownership and intended to demolish the house to make way for a highway overpass. Determined to preserve the historic structure, a grassroots movement, led in great measure by the Ramsey

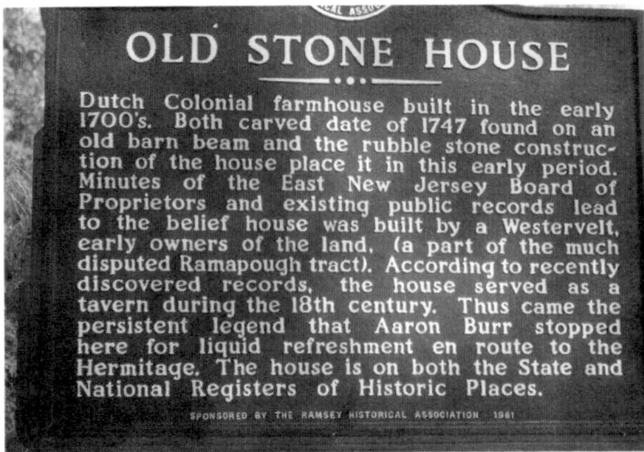

Left: Plaque with the history of the Old Stone House.

Below: Ramsey's Old Stone House sits forlornly on a slight rise. Built in the early 1700s, it served as a tavern in the later part of the eighteenth century. Legend has it that Vice President Aaron Burr stopped here, perhaps on his way to the Hermitage.

Women's Club, took the state to task and ultimately prevailed. Another piece of history was spared the bulldozer and wrecking ball.

The Dutch Colonial farmhouse today serves as a museum and is open to the public only on specific dates. (Check 201-327-2655 for information.)

The first floor of the museum holds period furnishings. Some of the original doors and frames are still intact. The floor also offers an exhibit on the military and an exhibit of a general store. A flight up displays children's toys and a period school setup.

In 1977, the house was placed on the National and State Registers of Historic Places. It was later recognized by the National Trust For Historic Preservation as a "Save America's Treasures" project.

19

REVOLUTIONARY WAR SITES

The following list is copyrighted by Al Frazza. Information is from Al Frazza's Revolutionary War New Jersey website, www.revolutionarywarnewjersey.com. Used by permission.

ALPINE

Palisades Interstate Park

Huyler's Landing

On the Hudson River

Huyler's Landing Trail

Begin at Alpine Lookout parking lot

The Kearney House

Near the Alpine Boat Basin

Closter Dock Road

Marker at corner of Old Dock Road

BERGENFIELD

South Church
150 West Church Street

CARLSTADT

Captain John Outwater Gravesite
720 Washington Avenue

CLOSTER

Nagle (Naugle) House
75 Harvard Street

Resolvert Nagel House
119 Hickory Lane

Nagel-Auryansen Cemetery
44 Susan Drive

CRESSKILL

Huyler's Landing Road Marker
East Madison Avenue and County Road

Site of Captain John Huyler's Farm
County Road and Linwood Avenue

Benjamin P. Westervelt House
County Road and Westervelt Place

DEMAREST

Sautjes Tave's Begraven Ground
Bogert Road and Everett Road

DUMONT

Old North Church Cemetery
120 Washington Avenue

Derick Banta House
Dumont Public Library
180 Washington Avenue

ELMWOOD PARK

Van Houten–Hillman House
891 River Road

EMERSON

Kinderkamack Historic Marker
Kinderkamack Road at Linwood Avenue

ENGLEWOOD

Liberty Pole
Lafayette Avenue and Palisades Avenue

FORT LEE

Fort Lee Historic Park and Visitor Center
Hudson Terrace

Monument Park
Palisade Avenue and Monument Place

Bergen County Retreat Route Signs
From Fort Lee Historic Park to Acquackanonk Bridge in Wallington

FRANKLIN LAKES

Franklin Avenue
Marker at 777 Franklin Avenue

GARFIELD

Post Ford Monument
River Road and Columbus Avenue

George Washington 1776 Marker
33 Outwater Lane

General Casimir Pulaski Monument
Riverfront Park
River Drive near Semel Avenue

HACKENSACK

The Green
Main Street and Court Street

Hackensack War Memorial
Main Street and Court Street

Burned Court House Site
Main Street and Court Street

General Enoch Poor Statue
Court Street at Moore Street

First Reformed Church
Gravesite of General Enoch Poor
Court Street at Moore Street

Archibald Campbell's Tavern Site
41 Main Street

Madison House Site
50 Main Street

Reformed Dutch Cemetery
Hudson Street near Lafayette Street

HARRINGTON PARK

Wortendyke Homesite
Schraalenburgh Road and Harriot Avenue

Blanch-Haring House
Lafayette Road and Hackensack Avenue

Old Burying Ground
Tappan Road and Arcadia Court

HAWORTH

Schraalenburgh Road Marker
Schraalenburgh Road

HILLSDALE

Garret Durie House
156 Ell Road

Westervelt-Demarest House
Hillsdale Avenue and Saddle Ranch Lane

HO-HO-KUS

The Hermitage
335 North Franklin Turnpike

LEONIA

Leonia Retreat Route Sign
Fort Lee Road and Oratam Terrace

Washington Retreat Monument
181 Fort Lee Road
In front of the Presbyterian Church

Van Horne's Grist Mill Site
Grand Avenue and Lakeview Avenue

Dutch Reformed Church Site
Hillside Avenue and Grand Avenue

Lafayette Encampment Marker
Fort Lee Road
Across from the library

Cole-Allaire-Boyd House
Grand Avenue and Prospect Street

MAHWAH

Ramapo Valley Road Marker
Ramapo Valley Road

Ramapo Valley Road Bridge
Ramapo Valley Road at Brakeshoe Place

Continental Soldiers Memorial Highway and W3R Markers
Ramapo Valley Road

Hopper Gristmill Site
156 Ramapo Valley Road

MAYWOOD

Revolutionary War Marker
Passaic Street and Maywood Avenue

MIDLAND PARK

Lozier House
Goffle Road and Paterson Avenue

NEW MILFORD

French Huguenot–Demarest Cemetery
Patrolman Ray Woods Drive

NORTH ARLINGTON

Pulaski Drive Marker
Pulaski Drive and Ridge Road

OAKLAND

Hendrick Van Allen House
Ramapo Valley Road and Franklin Avenue

Continental Soldiers Memorial Highway
Ramapo Valley Road

Jacobus S. Demarest House
Ramapo Valley Road and Dogwood Drive

ORADELL

Soldier Hill
Kinderkamack Road at Soldier Hill Road

PARAMUS

Paramus History Marker
North Farview Avenue—by Petruska Park

Old Spring Valley Burial Ground (Spring Valley Cemetery)
Spring Valley Way and Viola Way

Washington Spring Site
Van Saun County Park

Red Mill Site
Red Mill Road

Terhune-Gardner House
218 Paramus Road

George Washington Statue
George Washington Memorial Park
Paramus Road and Century Road

RAMSEY

Old Stone House
538 Island Road

RIDGEFIELD

English Neighborhood Reformed Church
1040 Edgewater Avenue

RIDGEFIELD PARK

Paulison-Christie House
8 Homestead Place

RIDGEWOOD

Old Paramus Reformed Church
660 East Glen Avenue

Historic Glen Avenue Marker
East Glen Avenue near North Maple Street

Abraham Godwin Monument
East Ridgewood Avenue and Van Neste Square
Ridgewood Municipal Park

RIVER EDGE

Historic New Bridge Landing
1201 Main Street

RIVER VALE

Baylor Massacre Park
Red Oak Drive and River Vale Road

ROCKLEIGH

Abraham A. Haring House
Peirmont Road near Rockleigh Road

Rockleigh Road Marker
Rockleigh Road near Piermont Road

TEANECK

Clarence W. Brett Park at Historic New Bridge Landing
River Road and Riverview Avenue

1780 Encampment Site
Teaneck Road and Cedar Lane

TENAFLY

British & Hessian Invasion Route
Tenafly Road

UPPER SADDLE RIVER

Old Stone Church Cemetery
481 East Saddle River Road

WALLINGTON

Acquackanonk Bridge
Main Street and Passaic Street

General Casimir Pulaski Monument
Main Avenue near Locust Street

WESTWOOD

Bogert's Mill Site
Mill Street and First Avenue

20

RIDGEWOOD

OLD PARAMUS REFORMED CHURCH

In 1725, the congregation of the Old Paramus Reformed Church was organized. In 1735, a church was built at the current location in Ridgewood in the Dutch Colonial style. In 1800, the congregation rebuilt the church using stonework from the original building. On the church grounds is a cemetery where some members of the original families of Bergen County lie buried. The Schoolhouse Museum is also located on the grounds. Across the street, one finds the Valleau Cemetery, where on many of the tombstones is inscribed a litany of the names of the founding families of Bergen County and the State of New Jersey.

The Old Paramus Reformed Church today.

The pews in the church were numbered, and members of the congregation were able to annually rent their seats. Slaves were allowed to be members and were seated in the upper galleries.

During the American Revolution, the church took an active role. The building and grounds were used by the Continental army for encampments, barracks, a hospital, headquarters of George Washington on several occasions and the site of the court-martial of General Charles Lee.

The church still holds regular services for the community.

SCHOOL HOUSE MUSEUM

Located somewhat in the center of Bergen County and bordered on the east by busy Route 17, Ridgewood is a community of civic-minded residents who have always had a love-love relationship with the borough. Upper middle class, there is an ethos of education and preservation of the locale's past.

In 1907, the Reverend Henry Cook, a newly minted minister just out of seminary, took over as pastor of Old Paramus Reformed Church. During his forty-five-year tenure there, he was a major factor in the creation of the Paramus Historical and Preservation Society, formed on February 11, 1921. To better describe the location of the organization, its name was later updated to the Ridgewood Historical Society.

In 1872, a small, one-room schoolhouse was built for village children at what is now 650 Glenn Avenue. Currently, it is the home of the Ridgewood Historical Society.

The Reverend Cook, a strong advocate of preserving local history, undertook the moving of artifacts that had been stored in his church to the then unused schoolhouse.

The School House Museum is currently organized and maintained by the Ridgewood Historical Society. The building is on the grounds of and rented from the Old Paramus Reformed Church.

The society's mission is to preserve the historic school building and maintain, interpret and exhibit the collection of artifacts representing the history, culture and lives of ordinary people from both the village and the surrounding area. Items dating from the period of the Native Americans to the early days of the twentieth century are presented in a consistently innovative manner.

The society mounts annual theme-based exhibits.

As with the schools of that era, boys and girls used separate entrances and sat on different sides of the room. There was a bell tower, since removed, where the rope to ring the bell was suspended by the girls' entrance. While the tower no longer exists, the bell rests near the entrance.

The exhibits are well laid out, and one feels comfortable moving from one to another. The School House Museum's exhibits are drawn from

The old schoolhouse is now a museum.

objects belonging to the museum as well as loans from local collectors and other sources as needed. There are docents on-site who are able to answer questions and are more than willing to engage visitors in conversation.

An example of the exhibits at the museum are artifacts focusing on the agrarian beginnings of Bergen County; there are many farm-related items. With some, there is a degree of controversy.

On April 1, 1807, New Jersey native David Peacock obtained a patent for an iron plow. This was a major innovation, as before this, plowing a field was backbreaking work for both men and animals.

Controversy erupted when he was sued for patent infringement by Charles Newbold of Burlington County in southern New Jersey. Newbold had obtained a patent for a similar plow in 1797. He won a judgment of $1,500 from Peacock but lost the war. Early farmers thought, for some unimagined reason, that Newbold's plow poisoned the soil and encouraged weed growth. Peacock's plow (Could he have stirred that pot? We will never know.) was taken to by the farmers, and they had their first labor-saving device.

The museum dedicates space to such history and has an exhibit of *Farm and Home* with artifacts from the eighteenth and nineteenth centuries.

The current exhibit emphasizes that art is not just for viewing in museums but has a firm basis in everyday life. On view are everyday objects: quilts, apparel, toys, furniture, hanging pictures, pottery and glassware. There is a curio cabinet containing examples of various types of photography dating from before the Civil War to the early 1900s. Lighting is provided to a large extent by hanging lamps, some antiques. In a separate room, there is an extensive collection of tools used by the farmers and craftsmen who built and populated Bergen County.

This museum is visitor friendly and will be well worth the time one devotes to visiting it.

Across the street is the Valleau Cemetery. It is interesting to walk through the grounds, reading the gravestones. One will view the final resting places of many members of the founding families of Ridgewood, Bergen County and New Jersey.

21
RIVER EDGE

HISTORIC NEWBRIDGE LANDING

A Scene from Yesteryear Today

On a sunny day in 1977, a local journalist was driving south on River Road in New Milford to participate in a radio broadcast at a nearby radio station. He suddenly pulled up short at an amazing sight: a house moving down the middle of the road.

New Milford, the birthplace of Bergen County, had given up one of its colonial-era treasures, the Campbell-Christie House, built in 1774 and residing in the borough ever since. The house was headed, slowly, down River Road to a new location: Historic Newbridge Landing in River Edge.

The County Historic Commission developed a site along the Hackensack River in an area bordered by New Milford, River Edge, Hackensack and Teaneck that would be a draw for history buffs from throughout the New Jersey/New York area and beyond. More importantly, homes dating to the beginnings of the United States of America would be preserved for untold generations to come.

As one of the major focal points of the colonies' war with the mother country, England, Bergen County has more sites in the National Register of Historic Places than any other county in New Jersey. Newbridge Landing Historic Park has become one of the more important destinations of our colonial history.

The Westervelt-Thomas period barn in the historic park.

Today there are four original colonial-era homes located at the historic park: the Steuben House, the Campbell-Christie House, the Demarest House and the Westervelt-Thomas Barn.

The preservationists succeeded in creating this small enclave of buildings that beautifully depict our past. Each has been meticulously preserved and would immediately be recognized by the original owner/occupants. They beautifully display examples of Dutch sandstone cottages, now an endangered style of architecture.

The (Von) Steuben House was built on land obtained by Jan and Annetje Zabriskie in 1745. Their purchase came shortly after construction of the original bridge at what is now known as New Bridge Landing. The bridge, a wooden drawbridge crossing the Hackensack River, was later a vital cog in the retreat of George Washington and his troops as they fled from capture by superior British forces, allowing them to safely regroup.

The oldest section of the Steuben House was the smallest, built in 1752 by the Zabriskies. It was considered a cottage. In 1767, the family added a second floor to the structure that more than doubled the existing number of rooms. It was topped off by a gambrel roof. A gambrel roof is like an upside-down *V* with a peak at about a thirty-degree angle. It can be seen today on barns and many common sheds. The style was then popular in much of the Dutch construction.

The (Von) Steuben House was now what the colonials would have considered a mansion. It boasted twelve rooms. There were adjacent buildings that served as a bake house, a smokehouse and a coach house. There were also two large barns and a beautiful garden. Two orchards covered some forty acres.

Unfortunately for them, the Zabriskies were Tories and supported the British. As a result, they left the property and fled to Manhattan.

George Washington, ever on the lookout during the war for a place to hang his tricornered hat and establish a headquarters, found the Steuben House to fit his needs. In 1780, he occupied the premises for more than two weeks. The Continental army made camp in what today is Paramus's Van Saun County Park, wherein lies Washington Spring (see page 135). His troops set up camp in an area that reached through River Edge into today's town of Oradell, and the aptly named Soldier Hill Road commemorates their encampment.

The Von Steuben House earned the name it is known by today when the State of New Jersey confiscated the property, as was common with the

Large in size for the day, the Steuben House was presented by a grateful nation to General Baron Von Steuben for the critical help he provided to the upstart colonies fighting the British empire.

holdings of those who sided with the Crown. It was presented by the state to Major General Baron Friedrich Wilhelm Von Steuben, who had come to this country to help the rebels. Interestingly, it is the only house ever owned by Von Steuben, who, as a soldier, was always on the move.

While the baron did not regularly live there, it was occupied by Captain Benjamin Walker, his aide-de-camp. Von Steuben did make regular visits and spent summer retreats at the house, coming from his quarters in Manhattan.

The home was damaged during the war and after peace came about, Von Steuben restored the damaged building to the condition it is in today. In 1788 he sold it back to the Zabriskies.

The house was purchased by the State of New Jersey in 1928, and in 1939 the Bergen County Historical Society was invited to showcase its collection in the building. In 1944, the society purchased the surrounding eight acres to preserve the Dutch countryside. Today the society offers the house for rent for special events.

In the late 1970s, the property was occupied by a junkyard filled with cars, trucks and other assorted vehicles, all leaking oil into the ground. When the property was taken over, all the vehicles were removed and the land mitigated to remove the oil-soaked ground. Today it is a pristine green field that could have passed muster in the seventeenth century.

The Campbell-Christie House, built of sandstone, was originally located in New Milford and constructed by Joseph Campbell, a mason, in 1774. He lived there for a time with his wife, Altche Westervelt, also from a prominent county family. Some of their descendants still live in the immediate area.

Campbell served as a private in the Bergen Militia. The house was damaged during the Revolutionary War and later sold in 1795 to John Christie, a blacksmith.

John Christie's grandson J. Walter Christie was born there in 1865. He earned fame as the father of the modern tank. Christie developed the Christie Suspension System, which was used in many armored vehicles during World War II.

As with many buildings of its era, the house was threatened with demolition to make space for modern development. However, Bergen County had a strong sense of historic preservation, and the house was obtained by the Bergen County Historical Society. The society moved the house to its present location in 1977—giving a journalist driving behind it a sight not to be forgotten.

The Demarest House, a Dutch sandstone structure, was built in 1794. It was a rather small cottage with only two rooms, built by John Paulson, a

The Campbell-Christie House now located in the New Bridge Historic Park. It was uprooted and moved by flatbed truck from its original location in adjacent New Milford and brought to the park, thus saving it from developer's destruction.

The Campbell-Christie House loaded on a flatbed in New Milford for its short journey to the historic park in neighboring River Edge.

miller, who was married to Altie Ely. Also originally located in New Milford before being moved to its current location, it was situated next to the French Burial Ground.

The house offers a display of artifacts from the prominent Demarest family and is actually owned by the Blauvelt-Demarest Foundation. In 2009, a major restoration project repaired the house.

If the Westervelt-Thomas Barn has a slight odor of colonial beer, that is because Peter A. Westervelt built it in 1889 with timbers from an old house and a local brewery. It was originally situated on Ridgewood Road in what is now Washington Township. The Bergen County Historical Society was the beneficiary of a donation in 1954 by a farmer, Henry Thomas. The barn was deconstructed and rebuilt at the Historic New Bridge Landing site it now occupies.

The barn was restored as an agricultural museum in 2014, funded by a donation from the Blauvelt-Demarest Foundation. It now holds farm implements, artifacts and tools from the early days of the country. There are sleighs, carriages and a grain barrel carved from a large sycamore tree.

Straddling the Hackensack River is the bridge the park is named for, the New Bridge. A close look at the photo shows the pilings that supported the original bridge famed for providing a means of escape during Washington's retreat. The bridge thus earned the sobriquet "The Bridge That Saved the Nation." Washington was able to regroup and continue fighting.

A crude mound for cooking at the historic park.

There are also a working broom machine and a bell from the old county courthouse.

Without the relocation of the colonial-era buildings, New Bridge Landing itself played a role in history. In 1774, a new bridge with a sliding draw to allow for the passage of ships was constructed. During Washington's retreat from the Fort Lee area on November 20, 1776, the Continentals crossed the bridge to safety.

Thomas Paine wrote of the event: "Our first object was to secure the bridge over the Hackensack." The bridge itself was the object of continued conflict, as it was the first bridge north of Newark Bay, a distance of about twenty-four miles.

The wooden bridge burned and was replaced in 1889 with a truss swing bridge that allowed ships to pass. It was so perfectly balanced that it could be opened by one person to permit ships to pass. It was closed to vehicular traffic in 1956. It is listed in the National Register of Historic Places as the oldest highway swing bridge in New Jersey. It no longer swings, and ships do not ply the silt-filled river anymore.

In its heyday, the landing was a narrow site built of log cribbing in 1744. Sloops of up to forty tons of cargo could go upriver. Today there are wood pilings around the steel bridge that may be from the original construction.

During the war, the landing site served as a battleground, fort, encampment, military headquarters and intelligence gathering post. There were some fourteen thousand colonial soldiers camped throughout the area.

The Continentals fled ahead of an onslaught by General Lord Cornwallis, who had crossed the Hudson River and attacked the lightly manned garrison at Fort Lee. Washington led his troops across Bergen County and across the New Bridge, saving his army from entrapment.

Notables in American history who were also at New Bridge Landing include the Marquis de Lafayette, General Henry Knox and artillery captain Alexander Hamilton. Hamilton, a native of the island of Nevis in the Caribbean, was promoted to lieutenant colonel and appointed aide-de-camp and secretary to Washington in 1777.

The Historic New Bridge Landing Park Commission was established in 1995 by the state. It tied together the towns of New Milford and Teaneck, Bergen County, the Historical Society and the New Jersey Department of Environmental Protection.

Editor's note: Coauthor Bob Nesoff, then a councilman in New Milford, was appointed a commissioner as that borough's representative to the founding New Bridge Landing Park Commission, serving as one of the members of the first board of commissioners.

22

RIVER VALE

BAYLOR MASSACRE SITE

During the Civil War, General William Tecumseh Sherman said, "War is hell." In any conflict, often both sides are guilty of atrocities. Almost a century before Sherman uttered those famous words, a group of Continental soldiers typified both the hell of war and the terrible atrocities it brought.

Throughout the ages, British soldiers have been known for the cruelty they brought on enemy military and even civilian sympathizers of their opponents. That vicious cruelty came to the fore in River Vale when they set upon a group of Americans known as Baylor's Dragoons.

The dragoons had quartered in barns on the coincidentally named Overkill Road, today's Rivervale Road in the hamlet of River Vale. The error made by Colonel George Baylor in not vetting the owners of the barns proved fatal to his troops. The barns were on farms owned by Tories, British sympathizers. While Bergen County was primarily populated by Patriots, there were hotbeds of Tories throughout.

One of the Tory farmers saw his chance to serve King George and hastened to the encampment of British troops.

Unknown to the colonials on September 22, 1778, Major General Sir Charles Grey, Major General Lord Cornwallis and Brigadier General Edward Mathew had been ordered to mobilize troops with the intent of provoking General George Washington into a battle. It would also serve as a diversion for a raid against a Patriot base in the southern end of New Jersey.

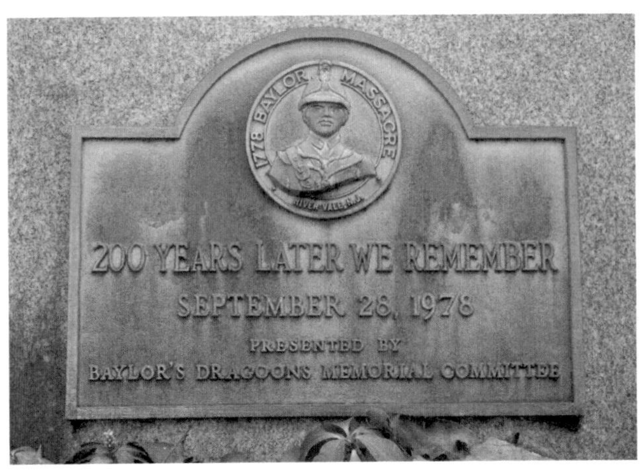

Remembering the massacre of Baylor's Dragoons—as they slept in a barn—by British troops. The redcoats shot and bayoneted the sleeping Continentals.

The British, thanks to the Tory farmer, were made aware of the presence of Baylor and his dragoons. Baylor had quartered his men in the barns and gave them the opportunity to sleep and earn some much-needed rest. He was in command of 104 enlisted men and several officers.

General Cornwallis waited until nightfall on September 27, and then at about 11:00 p.m. he began to move his troops into River Vale. Major General Grey, at Cornwallis's orders, mobilized the Second Battalion of light infantry and the Second Regiment of Grenadiers under his command. He was also given the Thirty-Third and Sixty-Fourth Grenadier Regiments.

Sometime between 1:00 a.m. and 3:00 a.m. Major Turner Staubenzie began to move six companies of light infantry. They joined with another six companies of light infantry under the command of Colonel John Maitland. The British began to silently approach the cluster of farmhouses and barns where the colonial soldiers were asleep.

In the barns were some one hundred troops belonging to a Virginia cavalry unit called Mrs. Washington's Guards. Colonel Maitland was assigned to cut off any night patrols as Major Staubenzie entered the barns and caught the colonials asleep. They methodically began to bayonet the surprised Americans and then moved from house-to-house killing any colonial soldier they came across.

Of the dragoons, about sixty were killed, seriously injured or taken prisoner. The British killed eleven on the spot and left four to die of their wounds. Colonel Baylor and three of his officers attempted to escape. Baylor was seriously wounded in the attack. He was captured and died in 1784 as a result of the lingering wounds. Another officer was bayoneted and killed while a third was captured.

Several of the injured colonials were taken to the Reformed Church of Tappan, across the street from the Old '76 House Tavern (see page 21). They were kept prisoner in the church that served as both a prison and a hospital. The church and tavern both stand today across from each other in Tappan, New York.

The British Fifty-Second Oxfordshire Regiment of Foot, nearing the end of its service in the colonies, was also put into service in the massacre.

British General Hunter wrote:

> *While at New Bridge we heard of their* [colonial soldiers] *being within twenty-five miles of our camp and a plan was laid to surprise them. We set out after dark, mounted behind dragoons, and so perfectly secure did the enemy think themselves that not even a sentry was posted. Not a shot was fired, and the whole regiment of dragoons, except a few who were bayoneted, were taken prisoner.*

Interestingly, this attack was considered a diversion for a later attack on American forces in Little Egg Harbor, about 138 miles away. British troops mounted an attack on October 15, 1778. Colonial troops under the command of Kazimierz Pulaski killed some twenty-five to thirty men in what became known as the Little Egg Harbor Massacre.

In Bergen County, the remains of Baylor's Dragoons killed in the raid were taken to three tanning vats alongside a stream and dumped. The vats, belonging to Haring's Tannery, were closed up and a large millstone covered the site. Years later, the millstone was removed, and the site was lost to history.

Skip forward 189 years, and a group of young collegiate amateur archaeologists began to track down the site of the burial in River Vale. Time was of the essence, as happens in so many instances involving historic locations. Housing development was planned for the area where the dragoons were suspected to have been dumped into the tanning vats.

Without the millstone, the precise location was anybody's guess. The youngsters, working with then Bergen County freeholder Bennett Mazur—literally on their hands and knees, using soft brushes and even toothbrushes—scoured the suspected location inch by inch.

Mazur drove from River Vale to the county courthouse in Hackensack, where newspaper reporters worked out of a ground-floor press room. He burst into the common office shouting about an amazing find. He looked around, and there was only one reporter in the press room. But that

"THIS MILLSTONE IS THE ONLY VISIBLE MARKER OF THE BAYLOR MASSACRE IN EXISTENCE TODAY. ON SEPTEMBER 28, 1778, A DETAIL OF BAYLOR'S CONTINENTAL DRAGOONS CAMPING AT HARING'S TANNERY IN RIVER VALE WAS BETRAYED INTO THE HANDS OF THE BRITISH BY A TORY AND SEVERAL WERE SLAIN. THE BODIES OF THE DEAD SOLDIERS WERE THROWN INTO THREE VATS AT THE TANNERY AND THIS STONE WAS PLACED OVER THE VATS TO HIDE THE BODIES. MANY YEARS LATER, GARRETT HOLDRUM'S FATHER DRAGGED THE STONE TO HIS HOME WITH A PAIR OF OXEN. LATER, GARRETT HOLDRUM, WHO WAS PRESIDENT OF THE SCHOOL BOARD FOR SOME SCORE OF YEARS, PRESENTED THE STONE TO THE BOARD OF EDUCATION AND, IN 1953, IT WAS MOVED TO THE SCHOOL WHICH BEARS HIS NAME."

PRESENTED BY
THE GRADUATING CLASS OF 1956
OF THE RIVER VALE SCHOOLS

Bergen County historians have placed informative plaques throughout the county at numerous historical sites. This plaque provides details of the murder of the Continental soldiers. It notes that a huge millstone was placed over the burial site. It was later removed, and the site was lost for more than two centuries.

Monument on the spot where the bodies of the Continental soldiers were uncovered centuries after their bodies were unceremoniously dumped into a tanning vat near a stream.

The millstone, with a marker, sits just feet behind the burial site. It was retrieved from a local school and placed in the park.

reporter worked for the biggest and most influential newspaper in New Jersey, the *Newark News*. The reporter looked at the red-faced and excited Mazur, trying to understand what Baylor's Dragoons were and of what importance.

The freeholder finally convinced the reporter to follow him to River Vale and see for himself. At the site, the young archaeologists were carefully brushing away dirt that had covered the spot since the day of the massacre. They slowly and carefully began uncovering shoe buckles, uniform buttons, pieces of uniform and bones.

They had uncovered pieces of rotten wood, indicating that this might have been the location of the wooden tanning vats. Slowly, carefully and reverently, they began digging through the packed earth until they struck historical gold. Mazur, sensing the opportunity for a newspaper story, headed to Hackensack looking for journalists and returned with the lone reporter.

The developer offered a parcel of land to the county, and it was turned into a county park. On October 15, 1972, it was dedicated and preserved for the future. The remains of the dragoons mercilessly killed while asleep or shaken aware by the British soldiers were reinterred at the Old Dutch

Church in Tappan. The millstone was recovered and is on display behind the semicircular monument to the colonial soldiers.

At the site, the county dedicated a plaque that reads:

> *In memory of American soldiers killed during the Revolutionary War in the "Baylor Massacre" on September 28, 1778. Lt. Col. George Baylor's 3rd Regiment of Continental Dragoons took quarters during the night on several nearby farms. Tories betrayed their presence to a British force who surrounded the Dragoons during the night. A number of Americans were killed or wounded after they surrendered.*

23

RUTHERFORD

OLD BAPTIST CHURCH

Admitted a Black Servant as a Member

In organizing the first Baptist Church in what was Boiling Spring, now Rutherford, the family of Richard Shugg invited its faithful servant, an African American named Cornelia Potter, to become a member. Richard Shugg had offered Sunday School lessons to neighborhood children, regardless of color. In this period, the late 1860s, there were no Black churches in Boiling Spring.

This first Baptist Church built its chapel in 1870 on a piece of land on Highland Cross gifted by Richard Shugg. The architect, Elisha C. Hussey, who was a member with his wife, Cecilia, offered the design for the wood-frame chapel. Much of the lumber to build the church was donated by George B. Holman, who operated his upholstery business on Newell Avenue. This is the same Holman family that located at 151–53 Park Avenue, where it established an upholstery and warehouse business in 1887. Remarkably, much of the wood-frame Hussey-designed chapel remains intact inside the Holman warehouse complex.

This first Baptist church disbanded after about fourteen years. A historical sketch of the Rutherford Baptist Church states the following: "On January 22, 1885, Mr. Richard Shugg gathered his family, Miss Cornelia Potter, their faithful Mammy, and a neighborhood family together and formed the Pilgrim Baptist Church and Sunday School." With its membership

The First Baptist Church was one of the first religious institutions to admit a Black congregant. The remnants of the church are still there but encased in a building hosting a commercial property.

increased to about sixty-four, the church relocated and built a church on a plot of land on West Passaic. It outgrew this small church, and in 1916, the Rutherford Baptist Church dedicated its current church at 23 West Passaic Avenue.

The church's stained-glass windows present a remarkable and lasting memorial to many of the congregation's founding members. These special windows, crafted by Flack Art Glass Works of New York, include one for Ida A. Shugg, Richard and Marie Shugg's daughter, who died on September 27, 1889, just nineteen years after the first chapel was built on Highland Cross. Across the chancery from Ida's remembrance window is an equally beautiful stained-glass window dedicated to Cornelia Potter, the faithful servant.

CASTLE BUILDING

Felician University Students Can Play Royalty

The halls of academia may often lend themselves to upper society, but students of Rutherford's Felician University can spend their time fortified in an actual castle.

First built in 1868 by Lloyd W. Tomkins, what was to become known as the Castle Building was meant to be his home. Tomkins, a newspaperman, land developer and entrepreneur, lived there for a scant nineteen years and christened the building the Hill House.

In 1887, it was sold to David Brinkerhoff Ivison, who was head of the American Book Company. Ivison began a major renovation of the building and turned it into a three-story turreted mansion. There were twenty-five rooms, including a music room—after all, what mansion is complete without a music room? The building began to take on the look of a Victorian castle. Ivison rechristened his magnificent structure Iviswold.

But Ivison didn't stop there. He had the money, and he was going to use it to create a unique structure that would stand out in the upper-middle-class town of Rutherford. He added a carriage porch and years later installed an indoor pool—of all places, on the building's second floor—with a water tower built into the structure to supply water for the pool. The only remnants of the natatorium can still be seen today. Ivison enjoyed his Castle until his death in 1903.

The home was a two-story structure with a mansard roof. Later work on the building added a third story, balconies and a porte-cochere. The exterior

Historic Castle Building on the campus of Felician University. It previously had been part of Fairleigh Dickinson University's Rutherford Campus.

walls were constructed of local brownstone. The structure was inspired by the Château de Chaumont in France's Loir-et-Cher region.

After Ivison's death, the Castle was sold several times and for a period of time was occupied by the Rutherford Union Club. In 1930, it was acquired by the Rutherford National Bank. The headman at the bank was one Fairleigh Dickinson Sr. Dickinson had a surfeit of wealth as the co-founder of Becton-Dickinson, one of the major pharmaceutical companies in the world.

In 1942, with major support from Dickinson, Fairleigh Dickinson Junior College was founded with Peter Sammartino as its head. The school took over the Castle Building and established its campus around the structure, with major expansion through the 1970s. The school later expanded and reinvented itself as Fairleigh Dickinson University (FDU) and moved its main campus to Teaneck. Rutherford continued as a sub-campus with the Castle building in daily use.

The Castle was used by FDU for classrooms, becoming more of a school than a residence. The rooms were reconfigured with drop ceilings and wall partitioning to create more classroom space.

As the university continued to expand and enroll a larger student body, it opened campuses in Teaneck and (now its main campus) Madison, New Jersey; Canada; the United Kingdom; and in the U.S. Virgin Islands with an underwater facility.

It soon became evident that the Rutherford campus and the Castle were superfluous to FDU's continued expansion and operation, and the campus and buildings were closed in 1994. It was later sold to a small nearby school, Felician College (later Felician University), which was expanding and found both the Castle and surrounding campus met its needs. In 1997, Felician purchased the property.

Felician had more of a sense of the history of the building and, after moving in, set out to restore the Castle to its former self. It is now the site of the school's offices. With renovations completed in 2013, the music room served as a chapel for Mass held by the Catholic institution. And while Felician University moved its operation to this campus and permitted visitors to enjoy the historic site, it is now closed to any but students, faculty and staff—and perhaps some invited guests.

In 2004, the Castle was included in the National Register of Historic Places.

The Felician renovation ran into an estimated $9 million over a fourteen-year period. And just as in the movies where uncovered treasure is found, historic relics came to light. Many architectural artifacts were there, as was a replica of an Italian frieze; intricate stained glass and a chandelier were found hidden behind the modern drop ceiling.

But there was more. There were raccoons.

The Castle had been in disuse and lacked maintenance or repair from 1994 until Felician purchased it three years later. And yes, raccoons had taken up residence in the building.

The eighteen-thousand-square-foot building leaked, causing mold, and the upper levels where the raccoons lived were a mess. In 1999, Felician brought in Historic Building Architects—a firm from Trenton, the state capital—to supervise the work. The firm was well versed in historic preservation.

To redo the interior ran to \$6.5 million. There was an additional \$2.5 million for the exterior of the building. The New Jersey Historic Trust and the Bergen County Division of Cultural and Historic Affairs wanted to help and contributed \$1.55 million for the restoration. Much of the remaining costs were covered by fundraisers and private contributions.

The Castle was featured in an article in *Scientific American* soon after it was built. The publication called it "a marvel of American Architecture," overlooking the French-inspired design.

When crews went to work, they found the aforementioned artifacts as well as grand arches and original woodwork hidden by layers of ancient paint. They reused whatever could be used to maintain as much of the historic value as possible. The crew did such delicate work that it was reported they filled several trash cans with Q-tips used in delicate cleaning.

Today, the renovated Castle hosts an admissions office, administrative offices and reception areas for on-campus activities. Some newer sections of the Castle are a dining area for students and workspaces.

But with it all, the school still remains a Catholic institution. High above the main hallway is a stained-glass skylight painted by Sister Ann Therese Kelly, who served as an art professor. The skylight is meant to remind those who enter that the school is a Roman Catholic institution.

While the original plan was to permit tours of the Castle, it is currently closed to all but members of the school's population.

24

TEANECK

OLD INDIAN BURIAL GROUND

Indians and Slaves Buried Off Pomander Walk...Maybe

For much of America's history, non-White people were consigned to burial grounds far from the rest of the population, and while some of them have disappeared to the pages of history, many are now covered by homes in bustling suburban communities.

Just east of the Hackensack River in Teaneck is an area considered to be the burial ground of both African slaves and Native Americans who lived in the area. The word *believed* must be used because there is no definitive proof that anyone is actually buried there.

Former Teaneck mayor and current councilman Elie Y. Katz invited this author to accompany him to the site. Katz, an avid protector of Teaneck's history and the remaining historic sites in the township, was eager to share any portion of local history.

Although there is a plaque near the curb indicating that this was a burial ground for those two groups, Katz said that could be in question. While locals are convinced it is a burial ground, he said there was no proof of such. When asked if ground-penetrating radar—a common instrument frequently used to locate bodies in crime scenes—would be brought in, he said no such plans were in the works.

The "burial ground" today is in a beautifully maintained field just off a single-family home subdivision. In fact, at one time, a house did sit atop the site. It is no longer there.

Slavery in the North, although not as common as in the South, still existed. This plaque tells that history.

A neighbor commented that when the home was standing, it was difficult to picture "what it was like back then." The neighbor, Dee Ann Ipp, a strong supporter of the site's preservation, commented: "Now you can see the real beauty of the land and why the Indigenous people chose this particular location for burials."

In 2009, after more than three years of legal back and forth, what has come to be known as the Old Burial Ground was saved from development. In October of that year, local officials signed a conservation agreement that provided an easement deed with the Meadowlands Trust.

That move transferred ownership of the site to the trust in perpetuity, saving it from developers. As is often the case in historic preservation, money changed hands. The trust gave Teaneck about $100,000 to offset the $400,000 the township paid a developer for the land.

The site is approximately 15,200 square feet. Lore says that Dutch settlers from the colonial era are buried there along with slaves and Indians. Preservationists and local historians point to township maps created prior to the 1960s that indicate the site was designated as a burial ground.

Then mayor Kevie Feit commented, "It was a long time coming. The burial ground represents not only different people and groups, but different time periods."

He was joined by former mayor Jacqueline Kates, in office when the site was originally brought to the attention of the governing body. Kates commented that residents from throughout the county had coalesced in efforts to preserve the site. They worked to save the property. She also

Left: The Teaneck Township Council placed a plaque at what has become known as the Indian Burial Ground on Pomander Walk.

Below: Teaneck councilman and former mayor Elie Y. Katz examines the descriptive plaque at the Indian Burial Ground.

pointed out that schoolchildren from nearby Dumont contributed pennies that they had collected.

In addition to funds from the trust and the children, college fraternities and sororities worked to raise funds for the preservation effort.

Katz, who was involved in the original preservation coalition, described saving the property as "one of the most meaningful projects I have been involved in with the township. The land is a wonderful riverside tract that is both beautiful and rich in history."

Ipp, who was central to the preservation effort, recalled seeing a mound on the site when she and her family move to Teaneck, living adjacent to the site.

"It was 1960, and I was a child," Ipp recalled. "I couldn't figure out what it was other than something that looked different than anything else. It was overgrown with weeds."

Wonderment turned to dismay later that year when developers came on the scene with their bulldozers and construction equipment. They leveled the mound.

She said it was a "great honor and special privilege" to have been able to take an abandoned and desecrated burial ground and return it to a state of reverence, sanctity and wholeness.

But while the preservationists celebrated their victory, the feeling was not unanimous. Tom Zabriskie, a direct descendant of the Zabriskies who lived in the area before the Revolutionary War, one of the most important settler families, contended the cemetery was part of Zabriskie-owned land extending from the Hackensack River all the way to Overpeck Creek.

Tom Zabriskie expressed the feeling that the cemetery was the burial ground for the Albert Zabriskie family and that there was no actual proof of slaves or Indians being buried on the site.

The land first aroused attention when a Hackensack dentist acquired the property with the intention of building a house alongside the river. That raised the ire of conservationists, who protested. They convinced the town council to purchase the property. It is believed that the part of the property closest to Pomander Walk contains remains. A stone marker was placed near the curbside commemorating the site as the burial ground.

Today, visitors can walk the property and enjoy the open manicured field and simply take in the history that has come down from the centuries.

25

TENAFLY

ROOSEVELT COMMONS

While "political correctness" has taken hold and monuments of "historically undesirables" are being removed or destroyed, even an equestrian statue of Rough Rider Teddy Roosevelt has been removed from a place of prominence in front of the huge American Museum of Natural History in New York City. But Tenafly has taken a different approach—respect.

Theodore "Teddy" Roosevelt, the twenty-sixth president of these United States, had a reputation as a big game hunter and leader of the Rough Riders charging up San Juan Hill in Cuba during the Spanish-American War. But while his reputation was intact, a monument dedicated to him faced a much worse fate.

In a park called Roosevelt Commons across from the municipal fire department stands a monument to his deeds and memory. But over the years, vandals have left their mark on the beautiful monument. The years took their toll as well.

Today there is a fence surrounding the bas-relief monument to keep these interlopers at bay. A stone carver and sculptor, Bob Carpenter, is slated to do the renovation work on the monument. The Tenafly

Opposite: The Borough of Tenafly dedicated a park to the memory of Rough Rider and President Theodore Roosevelt.

This page: Monument to Teddy Roosevelt in Tenafly's Roosevelt Commons, fenced off as repairs will be underway. The monument depicts the Rough Rider on horseback and animals he shot as an avid sportsman.

Historic Preservation Commission is supervising the restoration of the Indiana limestone monument.

There will be new decorative lighting installed by a New York firm, Focus Lighting. Karen Neus, commission chair, commented that she was "very excited" to be getting to the point of beginning the project. She noted that anything outdoors and subject to the elements will eventually need to be repaired.

The cost of the work, estimated at $125,000, is being split between Tenafly and the Bergen County Open Space, Recreation, Floodplain Protection, Farmland & Historic Preservation Trust Fund.

Originally completed in 1928, a creation of sculptor Trygve Hammer and his assistant, Fritz Hemberger, it has an arched top reaching a height of fourteen feet. The monument is two-sided, with Old Teddy on the front in bas-relief. There are carvings of birds and animals celebrating both his life as a hunter and preservationist.

The monument has a connection to Fair Lawn's Radburn section, discussed earlier, through Marjorie Sewell Caules, who designed the landscaping for both the monument and the Radburn PUD.

Malcolm Mackay, a wealthy philanthropist in Bergen County, gave the monument as a gift to Tenafly. His sister, Jennie Mackay, donated the twenty-eight acres making up what is Roosevelt Commons, today a favorite and relaxing parkland. The Mackays are remembered in the area for their generosity. The City of Englewood, next door to Tenafly, has a rather large urban park known as Mackay Park in their honor.

26

TETERBORO

TINY TOWN

Small Town, Big in History

Teterboro once held claim to being one of the smallest municipalities in the country. It consisted of eight single-family homes, twenty-two residents and a daytime population that ran into the thousands working in the Bendix plant and other commercial entities. Today it is home to sixty-seven people and tens of thousands of daily shoppers.

Teterboro came to prominence when, in 1917, Walter C. Teter took a muddy, mosquito-ridden piece of land and began to create an airport and a resort. Land was acquired from four surrounding municipalities to create the town.

The intent was to build an airport, golf course and commercial building. The airport was the only element to see the light of day. The first flight took off in 1919, piloted by Anton "Anthony" Fokker, who later designed aircraft used by Germany in both world wars.

As time progressed, commercial entities found Teterboro to be an attractive place to headquarter and were able to establish the municipality as a tax shelter. The Bendix Corporation became Teterboro's main industry, and at one point the name was actually changed from Teterboro to Bendix. That didn't last too long, as other corporations balked at the idea of using Bendix as their return address, and Teterboro made an official comeback.

Above: Where the major aircraft parts manufacturer once stood, the sign kiosk touts the shopping center.

Opposite: Big-box stores, restaurants and liquor stores now fill the spots where gyroscopes for the military were once manufactured.

But even with other firms safely ensconced in the municipality, Teterboro was somewhat akin to the old Spencer Tracy movie *Bad Day at Black Rock*. Bendix so totally controlled the town that the municipal administrator was, in fact, a full-time Bendix executive, and the mayor and councilmembers all worked at the plant.

In the mid-1960s, there were only eight private homes, no multiple dwellings and a population of twenty-two, most of whom were Bendix employees. The Watt family pretty much ran the show. The current mayor, John Watt, is the son of the late Delmar Watt, who was mayor from 1962 to 1997. His grandfather John Strunk was a councilman when the town was created.

While the population has increased minimally to about sixty-seven residents and additional housing units have been built, little else seems to have changed in the minute borough. John P. Watt is mayor, John B. Watt sits on the council and Mary Watt is the court clerk.

For a period of time, the county police patrolled the highway splitting the town in half. There is no longer a police chief. In fact, there is no longer

a police department. The police chief is listed in the county directory as "Moonachie Interlocal Agreement," meaning that an agreement has been entered into by at least two municipalities. Social and human services are provided by Bergen County. All of this is paid for by Teterboro.

Emergency management services are provided by neighboring Moonachie under an interlocal agreement. Councilman Gregory Stein is also chair of the land use board.

There was never a fire department. That was offered, if needed, by the airport or volunteers from Bendix. Today that is also provided by an interlocal agreement with Moonachie. And while there was once a board of education and a school board secretary for the town's two students, who attended school in neighboring districts, today's school superintendent position is provided by…yes…an interlocal agreement with another neighboring town, Hasbrouck Heights. Moonachie couldn't get everything.

So closely were things controlled that when a reporter for the local daily newspaper arrived with a photographer to do a feature story, they ran into the *Black Rock* treatment, reminiscent of the movie.

It was a sunny and bright day. Several children were playing in the street; windows and doors were open to the fresh air.

The photographer, driving a vehicle with the newspaper's name emblazoned on its doors, went to work putting his equipment together. When the reporter and photographer turned around, the children were gone, the doors and windows firmly shuttered and no signs of life. A knock on the doors of several dwellings brought no response.

The two journalists put their gear together and drove to the municipal building on busy Route 46 that bordered the Bendix plant. After they explained to the municipal clerk, Margaret Cahill, what their mission was, she called the administrator at his office in Bendix. They were told to "sit tight" and wait a few minutes.

Before they could relax, virtually the entire population of Teterboro began trooping up the steps of the municipal building for the interview. That was the epitome of the control Bendix wielded over the town and its resident-employees.

Municipal meetings are required by state law to have set dates, and those dates must be publicly posted to permit residents and whomever else would like to attend to know what, when and where the meeting will be conducted. The daily newspaper reporter arrived at the municipal building early for the posted council meeting. The building was dark, and no one—council members, clerks, anyone—showed up. When Mayor Delmar Watt was questioned, he said, "Oh, you must have gotten here late. It was a very brief meeting." In fact, the meeting was never held, and the "Bendix Syndrome" was in full play.

Hardly a high-crime area, Teterboro was told by the county to hire a policeman. It did exactly that: one policeman, Freddy Bolander. When he asked for a raise, the town promoted him to sergeant, and ultimately, after more raises and promotions, he was made chief of police. Bolander wore stars on his collar and scrambled egg on the visor of his hat, and he drove a police car with "Chief" emblazoned on it—chief of himself. To provide added help with traffic on the busy highway, Teterboro was told to hire a policeman. It did so from neighboring Little Ferry and made him a sergeant, and when Bolander retired, the sergeant became chief.

In the mid-'60s, State Assemblyman Vito Albanese attempted to introduce legislation abolishing Teterboro and returning the land to the towns it had come from. Albanese's attempt went nowhere, as the power of the aviation parts corporation, Bendix, had tentacles that reached deep into New Jersey politics. Albanese said he was offered $50,000 to back away, but he refused to do so. Albanese was not reelected, and the legislation was never brought up again.

Bendix and most of the corporations are gone, replaced by a huge shopping center known as Teterboro Landing offering everything from major private club box stores such as Costco to a variety of eateries.

In World War II, the U.S. Army operated the airport. Fred Wehren then owned the facility and leased it to the Port Authority of New York and New

Jersey. It was later leased to Pan American World Airways. In 2002, the Port Authority took full control and has operated the airport ever since.

The airport has hosted many famous people. In 1954, entertainer Arthur Godfrey thumbed his nose at airport officials and buzzed the control tower as he flew by in his private DC-3. Unamused, officials suspended his pilot's license.

Then president Bill Clinton arrived at the airport in a helicopter on his way to Fairleigh Dickinson University for a speaking engagement. Movie stars frequented its runways because of its proximity to New York. Corporate executives found it to be a convenient arrival point for the same reason, as well as the corporate parks in northern Bergen County, only a stone's throw from the airport.

Today it is arguably the busiest general aviation airport in the country. Its northern boundary is busy east–west Route 46. Busier Route 17 running north–south is less than a mile off.

Walter Teter, Anton Fokker and other famous persons wouldn't recognize either the town or the airport.

AVIATION HALL OF FAME AND MUSEUM

Teterboro Airport, from Muddy Field to Major General/Corporate Airports

Walter Teter had a dream. He was going to take a muddy section of southern Bergen County and turn it into a bustling resort, corporate magnet and one of the best general airports in the country.

Part of his dream came true. After many fits, starts and some stomach-turning problems he created both a Lilliput of a municipality and one of the busiest airports in the country. Teterboro Airport is arguably the busiest general aviation airport in the country, home to private planes, a flight school and national and multi-national corporations that headquarter their flight operations at the Bergen County airport, a stone's throw from the business centers in not only Manhattan but also corporate office parks situated in the northern sections of Bergen.

While thousands of people daily trek to Teterboro Landing, many miss another star attraction, arguably one of the most underrated and interesting attractions in the region, the Aviation Hall of Fame and Museum. Tucked away on the eastern perimeter of the airport at the end of the road, it beckons visitors to its collection.

Ralph W. Villecca Sr., executive director of the New Jersey Aviation Hall of Fame and Museum, stands by a part of a jet fighter in the collection of the museum.

Founded in 1972 by the late Pat Reilly, who for a time was a public-relations representative for Pan American World Airways, the facility houses a unique collection of aircraft and other memorabilia from the early days of aviation to the space age. Its collection goes well beyond just Bergen County and covers aviation history throughout New Jersey.

The facility is dedicated to preserving the history and accomplishments of New Jersey in aviation. The first balloon flight in the Western Hemisphere took place in Deptford in 1793.

In 1919, the first flight was made from the airport, and in 1926 Colonial Air Transport, headquartered at Teterboro, became the first private company to deliver mail by air.

In 1930, Teterboro Airport was the location for Anton "Anthony" Fokker's passenger plane, then the biggest in the world.

An important part of the airport complex is the New Jersey Aviation Hall of Fame and Museum, located on the southwestern portion of the field. The nexus between the airport and the museum has been one of mutual accommodation.

In World War II, the U.S. Army operated the airport. Fred Wehren then owned the facility and leased it to the Port Authority of New York and New

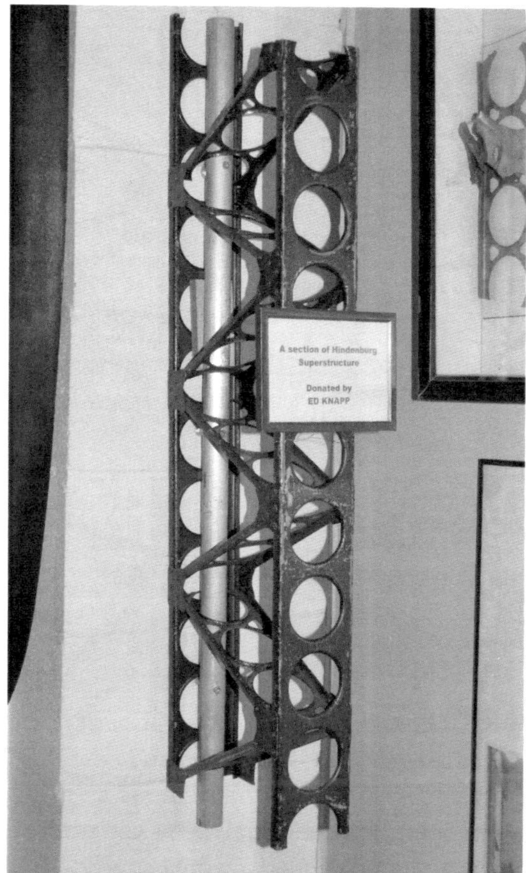

Right: An actual portion of a beam from the ill-fated airship *Hindenburg* that crashed and burned at the Lakehurst Naval Air Station on May 6, 1937, killing thirty-six passengers.

Below: A model of the *Hindenburg*, the largest airship ever built. It was more than eight hundred feet long. The pride of Hitler and Nazi Germany, it featured the swastika on its tail fins.

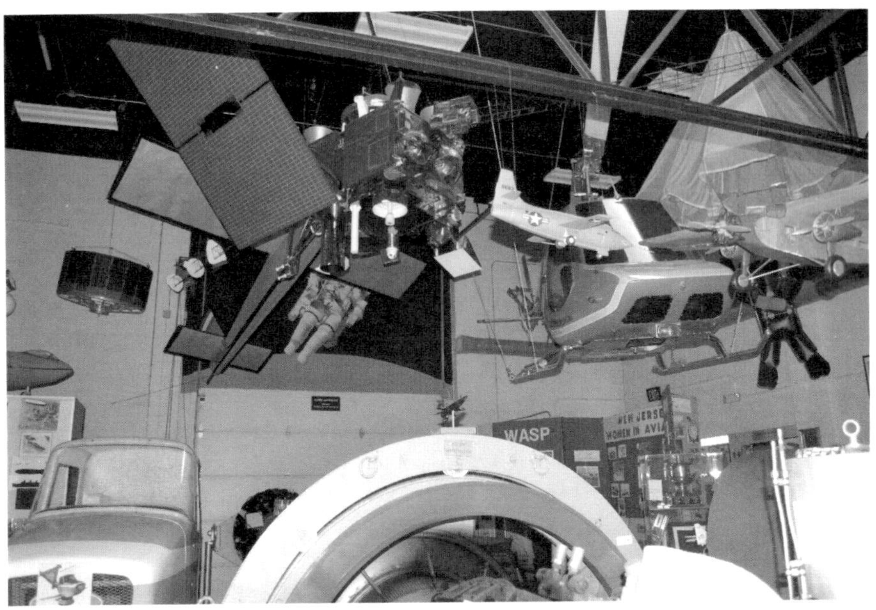

Aircraft and space suits on display hanging from the ceiling.

Jersey. It was later leased to Pan American World Airways. In 2002, the Port Authority took full control and has operated the airport ever since.

With all the history, what better place to locate a museum commemorating the history of Teterboro Airport and that of New Jersey aviation as well. At its founding the Hall of Fame and Museum was located in an unused radio tower. It subsequently moved in 1985 to a larger building and in 1997 to its current location.

In the museum's Hall of Fame is a plaque dedicated to Oradell native Walter "Wally" Schirra, one of the original Mercury 7 astronauts. Schirra passed away in 2007. Nearby is another plaque honoring Edward Eugene Aldrin, better known as "Buzz," the second human being to set foot on the moon. Aldrin, born in 1930, is a native Jerseyan.

The museum is a living entity with an opportunity for hands-on activity, especially with groups of Scouts. There is even an overnighter, Night at the Museum, for them on scheduled Fridays to Saturdays. Participants enjoy Friday night dinner, snacks, a "How to…" space presentation, a guided tour of the hall and museum and a scavenger hunt. Saturday morning starts with breakfast and then open cockpits of some of the aircraft and a fire truck for the Scouts to explore. For Scouts looking to earn rank, they can combine the program with qualifications for a merit badge. The staff for the program are volunteers who were, for the most part, involved in aviation and some from the military.

Guests of all ages have the opportunity to go into several of the exhibits and pretend to be flying over enemy territory.

The Dare to Fly program has a minimum requirement of fifteen students and introduces participants to basic aerodynamic theory. It includes a tour of the museum and is taught by experienced pilots and educators. The participants design and build their own gliders from raw materials provided for them. They then hold a flight competition to test the gliders. It is designed for eight- to fifteen-year-olds and is a comprehensive four-hour program.

Just looking for some fun? The facility offers the opportunity for groups to come in and enjoy hands-on exhibits with a private guide. There is a Fundamentals of Flight interactive aerodynamics exhibit that is operational and located in the Great Room. It was funded by a grant from the Dassault Falcon Jet Corporation.

On-site, the Hall of Fame and Museum displays historic aircraft, space suits and equipment, as well as artifacts such as a piece of the ill-fated *Hindenburg* that crashed and burned on landing at Lakehurst Naval Air Station, killing thirty-six passengers and crew.

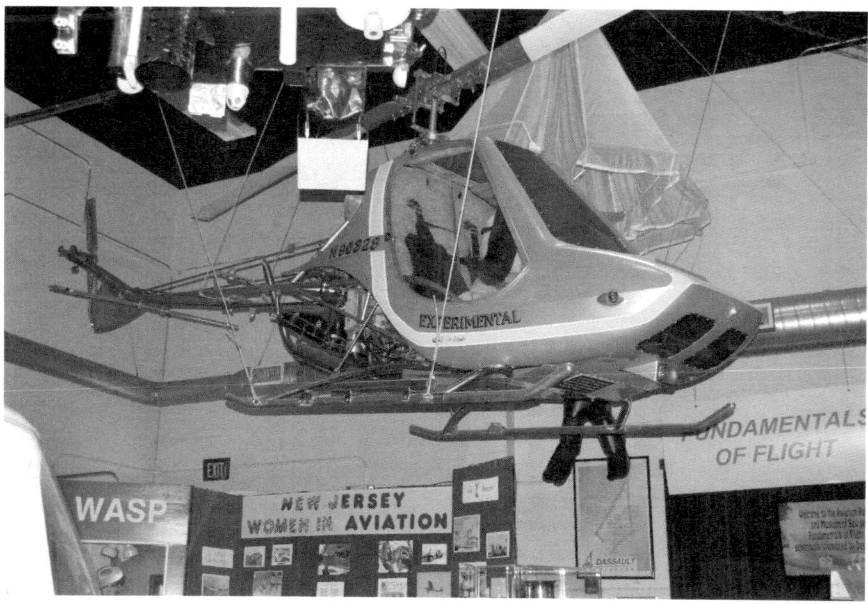

An experimental helicopter on display.

This page: Military aircraft on display on the museum's lawn.

Opposite: The famed workhorse vehicle of the military in World War II and Korea, the "Duece-and-a-half," the two-and-a-half-ton truck used as both a troop carrier and equipment transport.

On some weekends, visitors have the opportunity to actually fly in vintage aircraft over Bergen County and picture themselves on a bombing run in World War II.

The library boasts more than four thousand volumes on aviation history as well as a vast collection of videos. The facility's staff includes veteran pilots and aviation history experts.

Pat Reilly's successor, Ralph W. Villecca Sr., holds the titles of executive vice president and executive director of the facility. His knowledge of the Hall of Fame and Museum is almost boundless. When he takes a visitor on a tour, pointing out the history of almost every item in the collection, he does it with a reverence only outmatched by his respect. In fact, there are several pieces on display that have come from his own private collection, and Villecca is always on the lookout for more.

Many of those contributing time and expertise, guiding visitors through the extensive exhibits, are pilots. Stephen Riethof, a retired U.S. Air Force lieutenant colonel, is a certified flight instructor and frequently on hand to help guide visitors and describe the myriad exhibits in language any novice can understand and appreciate. There is also a cadre of volunteers who work diligently and regularly to ensure that the museum is inviting and in top-notch shape.

27

ORIGINS OF TOWN NAMES

INDIANS, DUTCH SETTLERS AND BRITISH INTERLOPERS ALL CONTRIBUTED TO MANY OF BERGEN'S TOWN NAMES

In 1972, a television producer was driving along the Palisades Interstate Parkway that winds its way along the eastern perimeter of Bergen County over the Hudson River and with an amazing view of New York City. It was a bright, warm day with a clear sky along the wooded roadway broken only by widely spaced exits and signs denoting the names of towns just past the off-ramp when a sign caught Barry Levinson's eye.

Next exit Tenafly.

Levinson slowed down as his brain began working overtime.

"What a name for a television show," Levinson thought. "Tenafly, a private detective."

In 1973, the TV show *Tenafly* made its debut as part of NBC's Wednesday Mystery Movie. It starred James McEachin as private eye Harry Tenafly, one of the early shows featuring an African American in the prime role. But while the show was named for a Bergen County municipality, it was set in Los Angeles.

The resemblance to the town of Tenafly came with Harry as a happily married man, middle-class, living in a suburban community when he wasn't fighting crime. That's where it ended.

Tenafly is a quiet municipality in the northeast-central section of Bergen County with a basically upper-income population, great school district, some shopping, a theater and a low crime rate.

The town was first settled by Dutch immigrants in the 1600s and incorporated by the State of New Jersey in 1894. The town's name is a derivation of the Dutch words *tiene vly*, loosely translated as "Ten Swamps."

As a heritage of the Dutch and British occupations, many of the county's names are an homage to their European origins. Bergen County itself may or may not have been named for Bergen-op-Zoom, a Dutch town from which many of its settlers came.

Other towns drew their names from the locations in which they were situated. Some are easy to determine: Bergenfield, as an example, had wide open fields. Consider nearby Cliffside Park, Englewood Cliffs, Fairview (overlooking New York) and Hillsdale in the hills.

Oakland had a profusion of oak trees, while Park Ridge is situated on a ridge. Oradell, home to the late astronaut Walter "Wally" Schirra, joins the Latin *ora* meaning "edge," and *dell* for its location at the base of hills.

Ridgewood is near a wooded ridge, and River Edge sits along the Hackensack River. The same holds true for River Vale, while Upper Saddle River has the river running through it. Could be a movie? *A River Runs Through It*?

Woodcliff Lake is near a lake in the woods. But Waldwick is Anglo-Saxon for "village in a grove."

Allendale is named for Joseph Warner Allen, an early surveyor in the area who came through in 1894. Bogota was a fur trading center and was named for the Bogert family, a prominent group of early Bergen County settlers.

Carlstadt, on the other hand, took the name of Carl Klein, who headed the German Democratic Land Association. Germans had a long history of settling in New Jersey and Bergen County in particular. In fact, prior to World War II, the German Bund had a location in what is today New Milford.

As with many designations, Closter has two competing derivations. One contends that it is from the English word *closter*, meaning "an enclosed place," while the more likely source is one of the first settlers, Frederick Closter.

Early settlers named Demarest or, as they were originally called, des Marets, still populate much of Bergen County. So why should they be left out? The borough of Demarest is said to honor David des Marets, a French settler who owned land along the Hackensack River.

Dumont Clarke, a New York banker, was the first mayor of the town named for him—Dumont. Emerson, originally Etna, honored poet Ralph Waldo Emerson, while Garfield is named for President James A. Garfield, assassinated in 1881. Washington Township is obviously named for the first president.

The Emerson Hotel in the late 1800s.

Harrington Park remembers one if its early settlers, the Harring family, while Haworth is named for the home of the Brontë sisters. You might think Franklin Lakes remembers old Benjamin, but while he was flying his kite, the town fathers honored his son, William, the last royal governor of New Jersey, no doubt a situation of chagrin for the Pennsylvania Patriot.

Ramsey is named for the Ramsey family, Rutherford for land promoters in 1870 honoring one of their own, John Rutherford. Teterboro, as noted elsewhere in this book, took its name from Walter Teter. Wallinton, once and always an enclave of Polish immigrants, drew its name from a seventeenth-century landowner, Walling Van Winkle.

Indians who populated the area before losing out to the hordes of European settles are remembered with town names such as Ho-Ho-Kus, the Lenape word for "brook." Hackensack, the county seat, remembers the tribe called Achensachys. Teaneck may be from the Lenape word for "place of villages," while Mahwah comes from the word to describe "meeting place." Moonachie skips a bit out of the area to take its name from an Indian chief, and Old Tappan is named for a subtribe of Lenapes. Just over the border into New York's Rockland County, portions of which were once part of the entire Bergen grant, is simply called Tappan. Interestingly, in New Jersey the name is pronounced "Tah-paan," while New York residents refer to their town as "Tap-in."

Paramus, once described by then police chief Joe Delaney as the Indian name for "shopping center" because of the profusion of malls, actually means "Place of Wild Turkeys." Perhaps the same could be said today, when the place is overrun with Christmas and sale day shoppers.

The town of Norwood was a section of property bought from the Lenape that had been the "Northwoods." One of the more interesting and obvious town names is Glen Rock for its most identifiable landmark. Smack in the middle of town is a gigantic boulder. The Lanape called it the "Pammackapuka," meaning "rock from heaven." Glen Rock was easier on the tongue for the settlers. While today it is a meeting place for people, since you can simply say, "Meet me at the Rock," its history indicates the Indians did the same thing, using it as a meeting place. It sits today where it has been for thousands of years, in a circle in the middle of town.

Cresskill—break that into two words. *Kill* is Dutch for "river" or "stream," and watercress once was cultivated along the banks of the Tenakill Brook. Little Ferry, adjacent to Teterboro Airport, was once a launching site for a ferry in colonial days that ran from the foot of Mainstreet plying the Hackensack River when it was navigable.

The French influence still reigns with the town of Rochelle Park, named for LaRochelle, France. Maywood is an interesting enclave whose residents have termed themselves "Maywoodians." It derives its name from 1872, when landowners named a new depot "Maywood" and began laying out streets that now run through the town. The bucolic name was designed to entice new residents and businesspeople.

New Jersey's mix of municipalities could drive a cartographer mad. While most are incorporated as boroughs, two—Ridgewood and Ridgefield Park—are villages. Three are cities, the aforementioned Garfield along with Englewood and the county seat of Hackensack. Teaneck and Wyckoff are townships.

Englewood was the first to incorporate as a city, with a name that was created by its politicians. Its neighbor Leonia, home to many authors, entertainers and academics, has a tinge of mystery to its name. Some contend it incorporated a portion of Fort Lee, an adjacent town, while others are sure they simply don't know.

Wyckoff was originally the site of an Indian burial ground. But be that as it may, the name has nothing to do with the Indians. It comes from a town in England named Wicaugh in Malpas.

While most municipalities in Bergen County and throughout New Jersey trace their names back to early settlers, others do it to simply get away from what they consider to be an undesirable designation.

Passaic County's county seat of Paterson, one of the state's larger cities, has long had a reputation as a central point for gangs, drugs and crime. Not that many years ago, Paterson was a family-oriented municipality. It was a center for entertainment, dining out and shopping. Over the years, it suffered a downward spiral, and today its reputation is far from what it once was.

To honor their location, two municipalities, one in Bergen County and the other in Passaic County, bordering on Paterson, faced a dilemma. In Bergen County, the town was named East Paterson, while in Passaic there was West Paterson.

Given concerns about the connection to the city of Paterson and its inherent urban problems, name changes were offered up to the residents of both towns.

To say that there was opposition to such a change is to minimize the connection of many residents to what has always been. In Bergen County, East Paterson became the first to offer residents an opportunity and an option for a name change. The suggested new name was Elmwood Park, a more bucolic designation. The initials, E.P., would remain and negate the need to change signs and logos. With much controversy and consternation, the name was changed on referendum, and ultimately, most, if not all, residents embraced the new name.

West Paterson, in Passaic County, was next. The same opposition to changing what always was came to the fore. The proposed new designation was Woodland Park. Again, after much controversy and discussion, it went up on referendum, the initiative passed and West Paterson was consigned to the history books.

Some information comes from the Encyclopedia of New Jersey, *Rutgers University Press. Additional information comes from an essay by Michael Timko and yet more from the author's own files.*

ABOUT THE AUTHORS AND ACKNOWLEDGEMENTS

BOB NESOFF

Bob notes that unfortunately he lost his wife, Sandy, in January 2021 after a long marriage. The couple coauthored much of their work, especially their syndicated travel column, as they traveled the world together. Sandy began working on this project with Bob and Howard Cohn until she very unfortunately fell ill and ultimately passed away from brain cancer. Bob has dedicated his work on this book to his wife of fifty-five-plus years and the love of his life.

Bob Nesoff, coauthor, is a multi-award-winning career journalist who has worked for two major daily newspapers in New Jersey. He covered Bergen County for the New Jersey dailies and is personally familiar with many of the sites included in this book. Much of the information has come from his own files gathered over the course of his career. Bob was the only reporter present when the remains of Baylor's Dragoons were uncovered in a tanning vat in the town of River Vale after more than two and a half centuries.

As a reporter and newspaper editor, Bob has won more than forty journalism awards from several organizations. He was president of the Working Press Association of New Jersey and the North Jersey Press Association. He served as national president of the North American Travel Journalists Association.

In 2019, he was presented with the Albert Nelson Marquis Lifetime Achievement Award. He is a longtime member of the prestigious American

Society of Authors and Journalists (ASJA) and the Society of Professional Journalists (SPJ).

Bob was executive editor of *New York Lifestyles Magazine*. He was also a regular contributor to *Lifestyles Magazine* (not to be confused with *New York Lifestyles*), an upscale international publication, and travel editor for *Mohawk Valley Magazine*. He also served as travel editor for Urban Matter–New York, a major website covering much of the country. His articles have appeared in numerous publications such as Rand McNally, *San Antonio Express-News*, the *New York Times* and the *New York Daily News* and a host of outdoor magazines. Early in his career, he was an editor with CountryWide Publications with responsibility for a half-dozen sporting and outdoor magazines aimed at the men's market.

In 1998, he was named to Marquis Who's Who in America and Who's Who in the Media and Communications. He began his career with a weekly newspaper in New York's Rockaway section in Queens writing a column and covering local stories.

Bob and Sandy covered the launch of Apollo 17, the last manned moon launch. They reported from Croatia shortly after the shooting and bombing ended but were at the edge of a minefield as soldiers cleared the explosives. Over the course of their careers, they met a half-dozen astronauts, and Bob was selected as a candidate for the Journalist in Space program. That program was terminated after the tragic end of the *Challenger* mission that killed all aboard on launch, including schoolteacher Christa McAuliffe.

Bob was a nationally syndicated columnist for the former McNaught Syndicate writing a column that appeared in nearly one hundred newspapers across the county and currently writes a weekly travel column that for many years was coauthored by Sandy. The couple traveled extensively throughout the United States, Caribbean, Europe, Africa, the South Pacific and China. Bob is the author of the adventure novel *Spyder Hole*, which has garnered unanimous kudos from reviewers, and sold the movie rights to a Hollywood producer.

He is currently working on another book for this publisher, titled *Mysterious Mike Malone*, about the federal undercover agent who brought down Chicago crime boss Al Capone. Malone also was involved in the Lindbergh baby kidnapping case and investigated such other notorious figures as Dutch Schultz, Waxey Gordon and *Boardwalk Empire*'s corrupt politician Nucky Johnson.

Bob is familiar with undercover work. Because of his connection to the Federal Criminal Investigators Association, he was approached by a Mafia associate to help fix a tax case against a Mafioso. He reported the approach to the government and worked undercover with federal agents for almost a year. He was involved with the federal agents in the investigation until the Abscam case broke and scared the ciminals off. In his "free" time (whenever that happens to be), he enjoys skiing and is a past board member of the North American Ski Journalists Association. He is an avid SCUBA diver and has gone below the waters from New York to the Tahitian Islands.

Bob was founder of two charity motorcycle runs that raise funds for military and first responders seriously injured or killed in the line of duty. He himself was a first responder on 9/11 at Ground Zero, going in with the Bergen County sheriff.

THANKS FROM BOB...

A book of this nature would have been impossible to write without the assistance of many people. That holds especially true for a book on history and the people who made that history.

I'll say thanks here and now to all those mentioned below rather than do it individually. Each and every one of them paved the way for us to gather information on facets of Bergen County's history. This book covers a vast number of interesting locations, some dating back hundreds of years, while others are far more contemporary.

And while this is a comprehensive detailing of Bergen County, there are far too many locations and stories for one book. Bergen County has more sites designated in the National Register of Historic Sites than any other New Jersey county. And remember, Bergen County is considered the "Crossroads of the Revolution."

Washington's retreat route from New York cut through the heart of Bergen County. Aaron Burr had ties here as well. Many of their contemporaries, such as the Marquis de Lafayette and Alexander Hamilton, could have called Bergen home. And there was a connection to the worst case of treachery in the history of this country that tied Benedict Arnold to British spy Major John André.

While the Old '76 House now resides in New York's Rockland County, bordering Bergen, it was in the early days of this country part of New Jersey before permanent lines were drawn. Rob Norden, owner of the Old '76 House, was a wealth of knowledge about André and the plot to hand West Point over to the British.

David Zimmer, reporter for the *Record* daily newspaper and part of the USA Today network, was helpful in providing information about the old church in Garfield that was home to early African Americans and several other locations. From the same newspaper, reporter Marsha A. Stoltz was quite helpful in providing information and contacts for the piece on the grave of a dozen Revolutionary War soldiers in Oakland, "lost" for more than two and a half centuries. American Legion commander Ronald Beattie took time to meet there and offer information on the search for the exact location of the bodies and the very interesting way in which they were found.

A very special thanks must go to Robert "Bob" Ryan, former New Milford fire chief, who gave us access to a treasure-trove of historic photos of Old Bergen County from his private collection, with many going back well over a century. Those photos are interspersed throughout the book. In most instances, they are coupled with photos taken as the book was being written, in as close to the spot of the original pictures, giving an amazing comparison of "then and now," with some showing dirt roads that today are major paved roadways. The modern photos were taken by the authors.

Also, thanks to former Teaneck mayor and current councilman Elie Y. Katz for providing background information on the Indian Burial Ground in his town. The site is not well known and is marked by a stone at the curb near the entrance. But according to Katz, there are plans in the works to improve the site. A more prominent marker to honor the original residents of the county is under consideration.

Howard Cohn and I spent many hours and days and drove scores of miles taking the current comparative photos. But the display of old and new was well worth the time. Howard's knowledge of history was a great add to our research.

George Carter, the Oradell Borough historian, graciously lent books detailing the history of his town. We were able to trace the story of the historic Blauvelt Mansion that looms over Kinderkamack Road and the efforts to save it from what many in the town consider intentional neglect by the current commercial owner so that it can be replaced by a care facility. Efforts to obtain comment from CareOne, current owner of the mansion, were never responded to.

Much of the background and historical information came from my personal records. As a reporter for the *Record* and later the state's prime daily newspaper, the *Newark News*, I covered stories of historical importance and was the only journalist on the scene when the bones of the murdered Baylor's Dragoons were found during an archaeological dig in River Vale.

On a drive through Bergen County, a visitor will notice blue marker plaques designating historic sites. They are too numerous to count. A casual drive will bring you past stone houses hundreds of years old. They are in virtually every town and almost on every street. Most are still occupied. But please do not attempt to look in the windows or knock on the doors. For all you know, the current residents may have a loaded musket ready to take down strangers.

Wikipedia was a wealth of information, filling in gaps and providing details and history. I urge you to use that as a major resource. Several local historical committees added to our information.

A special thank-you to Al Frazza for information from the Revolutionary War New Jersey website, www.revolutionarywarnewjersey.com, created by Al Frazza and used by permission in this book. The site is copyrighted and extends with each passing year. Any other use of this information must be approved by Al Frazza.

Also, a special thanks must go to my late wife, Sandy Nesoff, who, while she was able, read copy, made suggestions and added considerably to the book. Her help and presence are sorely missed.

HOWARD JOSEPH COHN

Howard Joseph Cohn was born in the Bronx, New York. He earned bachelor and master's degrees in fine arts from CCNY and an MFA in printmaking from Herbert H. Lehman College, CUNY.

Courtesy of Susan Cohn.

He is a retired teacher from the NYC Board of Education, having taught for thirty-three years.

He served on the board of directors of the Bergen County Museum of Art and Science and on the executive board of trustees of the New Jersey State Museum. He was the president of the New Jersey

Paleontological Society and the Beth Tikvah Jewish Center, New Milford, New Jersey.

His writing skills were honed via articles written for the organizations he was a member of, as well as an extensive number of letters to the editor published in many newspapers and periodicals.

His abiding interest in history led him to collaborate with Robert Nesoff in researching and writing this book.

THANKS FROM HOWARD...

I take this opportunity to thank Bob Nesoff for asking me to join him in writing this book. He was aware of my interest in history, my writing abilities and how well we have worked together on previous projects. Our involvement with the research and activities connected with the work necessary to publish this tome only fed my curiosity and accumulation of knowledge.

There are a few other individuals whom I feel obligated to thank. The first is my wife, Susan; she read some of my articles before submission and joined me in many travels to investigate and visit locations included in this book.

My friend Glen Salsbury, a lifelong resident of Paramus, was a very knowledgeable source of many oral histories of this area. Driving with him as my guide opened my eyes to current historical sites still in existence as well as pointing out where some of those that have been destroyed were located.

Pandemic restrictions closed practically all of the local museums and houses that would have been open for visitation. Glen was able to recommend and introduce me to Joseph Suplicki of the School House Museum in Ridgewood. Suplicki opened the museum for us and shared his knowledge of the many objects on exhibit. We walked through the entire museum, with him answering all of my questions. The museum is on the grounds of the Old Paramus Reformed Church, and the pastor of the church, Reverend Robert L. Miller, was kind enough to meet with me and expand the information that I had concerning the early history of the church and the way of life of the populations who lived during those times.

My daughter Miri Upton introduced me to Tom Grissom of the Mahwah Museum in Mahwah. He guided us through the main building as well as the nearby Old Station Museum. Exhibits explained, queries made and knowledge shared, one couldn't expect more.

Father Dermot S. Roache, SMA (African Mission Society), walked with us through the African Art Museum in Tenafly, pointing out and explaining some of the art on exhibit. When I had questions that he could not answer, he had me call Father Frank Wright, SMA, to seek the information I sought. I returned to the museum, and my queries were subsequently answered by Father Wright.

My thanks go out to all of the others I came in contact with and the individuals who ceaselessly devote their time and energies to preserve the historic sites in Bergen County as well as in all other areas. More interest and efforts must be devoted to the preservation of our historic sites, rather than the continued destruction and development that has and will take place without resistance.